Dirt Track Auto Racing, 1919–1941

Dirt Track Auto Racing, 1919–1941

A Pictorial History

DON RADBRUCH

McFarland & Company, Inc., Publishers
Jefferson, North Carolina, and London

LIBRARY OF CONGRESS CATALOGUING-IN-PUBLICATION DATA

Radbruch, Don.
Dirt track auto racing, 1919–1941 : a pictorial history / Don Radbruch.
p.   cm.
Includes index.

ISBN-13: 978-0-7864-1725-4
softcover : 50# alkaline paper ∞

1. Automobile racing—United States—History. 2. Automobile
racing—United States—History—Pictorial works.   I. Title.
GV1033.R34   2004   796.72'0973—dc22   2003023694

British Library cataloguing data are available

©2004 Don Radbruch. All rights reserved

*No part of this book may be reproduced or transmitted in any form
or by any means, electronic or mechanical, including photocopying
or recording, or by any information storage and retrieval system,
without permission in writing from the publisher.*

Cover photograph: Joe Sostillio at Weymouth, Massachusetts

Manufactured in the United States of America

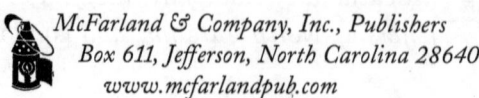

McFarland & Company, Inc., Publishers
Box 611, Jefferson, North Carolina 28640
www.mcfarlandpub.com

Acknowledgments

There is a "magic book" that forms the backbone of my research for this book: Allan Brown's *The History of America's Speedways—Past and Present*. This remarkable book provided starting points for most of the information presented here. Brown lists some 6,400 racetracks in the United States and Canada. His book is a necessity for anyone interested in racing history, and even the casual racing fan will enjoy browsing through it. The past and present tracks are listed by state and Canadian province. Some listings provide a short history of the track, while others have the simple notation, "Location and dates unknown." About a hundred photos accompany the text. The book was published in 1994—it is a safe bet that Allan Brown has found a thousand or so additional racetracks since then. A new edition is scheduled for release soon. *The History of America's Speedways* is a thoroughly fascinating book. I couldn't do without it—thanks for writing it, Allan! For more information, contact:

> America's Speedways
> P. O. Box 448
> Comstock Park MI 49321
> (616) 361-6229

The other essential source in the preparation of this book was Phyllis Devine's *The Alternate*. Directly or indirectly, this Pennsylvania-based publication provided most of the material and photos for this book. The articles in *The Alternate* provided a wealth of background material and basic information on racing in the 1920s and 30s. Best of all were the contacts with racing historians in the United States and Canada that came through this neat little magazine—there must have been at least a hundred of them. From these contacts came more information and more photos. It is safe to say that without *The Alternate* this book would not have happened. Thanks, Phyllis! For more information, contact:

> *The Alternate*
> Phyllis Devine
> P. O. Box 239
> Grantville PA 17028-0239
> (717) 469-0777

Acknowledgments

I found that people who had helped me with my roadster books were willing to help with this new project. They had friends who were willing to help. Publicity in *The Alternate* and in *National Speed Sport News* turned up more people. Scores of people lent me photos to copy—sometimes a whole album containing a hundred or more photos. Copies of newspaper clippings provided some basic information on the bigger races, plus data from obscure locations in the United States and Canada. The stack of photos and other material just grew and grew. Fortunately, a few of the 1930s racers are still around. They provided the most precious thing of all: first-person anecdotes from the past.

This book would not have been possible without the help of a hundred or so wonderful people. The following people helped immeasurably with this book. I hope that I have not left any of them out. Sadly, some of these fine people are no longer with us.

Art Abrahams
Richard Andre
Emil Andres
Bob Barkhimer
Mike Bell
Dave Boon
Buck Bowers
Ken Breslauer
Allan Brown
Wendell Bundy
Leroy Byers
Emmett Carpenter
Jim Chini
Myke Collins
Bruce Craig
Allan Darr
Phyllis and Joe Devine
Dick Downes
Mark Downing
Roy Eaton
Chris Economaki
Erwin Eszlinger
Joseph Evans
Dale Fairfax
Joe Fiore
Joe Freeman
Howard Gardner
Bob Garner
Joe Gemsa
Richard Gonsalves Jr.
Pike Green
Jim Haag

Phil Harms
Chuck Harring
Ray Hiatt
Bill Hill
Billy Horner
John Jackson
Walt James
Grace Jones
Warren Jones
Johnny Klann
Butch Knouse
Jim Knull
Perry Kratchmer
Loren Kreck
Galen Kurth
Bill LaRosa
Chick Lastiri
Bob Lawrence
John Levrett
Dave Lewis
Lew Lewis
Marty Little
Christine Horey Logan
Tom Luce
Earl Mansell
Jack Martin
Gordon McIsaac
Bob McMurtry
Frank Mikkelsen
Tom Motter
Jerry Murwaski
Bob Noe

Dave Norgaarden
Don O'Rielly
Harold Osmer
Al Powell
Brian Pratt
Terry Reed
Stan Reynolds
Spencer and Judy Riggs
Kem Robertson
Ralph Rogers
Rosie Roussel
Bob Rushing
Tom Saal
Doris Schindler
Bob Silvia
George Sowle
Bob Stolze
Bob Swarms
Paul Tainter
V. Ray Valasek
Dee Walsh
Les and Beryl Ward
Ed Watson
Jim Way
John Way
Tom Welch
Monte Wellendorf
Gordon White
Nelson Wierenga
Bill Wood
Crocky Wright
Charlie Yapp

Last, but certainly not least, is my wife, Naida. Her endless proofreading and corrections of my punctuation are greatly appreciated. Naida is an "in house" editor.

Contents

Acknowledgments	v
Preface	1
Introduction: Big Cars, Outlaws, and Midgets	5
1. Pacific Coast: *Washington, Oregon, California*	9
The Other Aggie	42
Ascot	43
Goshen, 1934	44
Oakland—500 Miles on the Dirt	45
Rajo Jack	50
Rex Mays	53
San Jose, 1924	56
Seattle	60
South Gate	61
The Chrome	65
2. Mountain States: *Montana, Idaho, Wyoming, Nevada, Utah, Colorado*	68
The Alan Track	77
Bonneville Speedway	78
Colorado Springs	79
Missoula, Montana	80
Noel Bullock at Pikes Peak	81
The Gardner Brothers	83
The WOIRA	86
3. Southwest: *Arizona, New Mexico, Texas*	88
AAA Racing in Texas	92
Albuquerque, 1927	94

The Bisbee Trophy	95
The First Stock Car Invasion	96

4. **Northern Plains:** *Minnesota, North Dakota, South Dakota* — 98
    - The Fronty — 109

5. **Central Plains:** *Nebraska, Kansas, Oklahoma* — 111
    - The Hatton and Hurst Circuit — 122
    - The Lawrence Hughes Collection — 122
    - The Kansas Cyclone — 127
    - The Musick Brothers — 130
    - Ord (by V. Ray Valasek) — 133

6. **Midwest:** *Wisconsin, Iowa, Illinois, Missouri* — 139
    - Ford V-8 — 153
    - Fred Frame — 154
    - The Indianapolis Oakland V-8 — 156

7. **Lake States:** *Michigan, Indiana, Ohio* — 158
    - Ben Gotoff — 176
    - Hammond and the Rim Riders — 178
    - Henry Meyer — 180
    - Larry Sullivan — 182
    - Mount Clemens — 182
    - The New Bremen Riot — 184
    - VFW Speedway — 184

8. **Northeast:** *Maine, New Hampshire, Vermont, New York, Massachusetts, Connecticut, Rhode Island* — 188
    - Bronco Bill — 202
    - The Joe Freeman Collection — 203
    - Myke Collins — 210
    - The First Super Speedway — 211
    - The Bentley — 213
    - The *Big*, Big Car — 214

9. **East:** *Pennsylvania, New Jersey, Maryland, Delaware, West Virginia, Virginia* — 215
    - Chris — 228
    - Central Pennsy — 229
    - "By J. Earl Way" — 234
    - The Match Races at Johnstown — 235
    - The Mysterious Mr. Chamberlain — 235
    - Troy Hills — 236
    - Williams Grove — 237

10. South: *Kentucky, Tennessee, Arkansas, Alabama, Mississippi, Louisiana*	241
Fred Horey	243
Shreveport, October 22, 1941	246
11. Southeast: *North Carolina, South Carolina, Georgia, Florida*	248
180 MPH	253
12. Canada: *From Sea to Sea*	256
Big Cars in British Columbia (by Brian Pratt)	266
Strange Shenanigans in Saskatchewan	267
On the Docks	267
The Midday Ride of Wes Moore	272
13. Those Pesky Midgets	274
14. The Way It Was	278
The First Racing Publication?	278
National Speed Sport News—The War Years	279
Best of the 1930s	283
Lady Racers	288
The National Championship Drivers of America	290
Creative Financing	291
Deal Money	292
Hippodrome	293
Real Dollars	293
Medical Aid	294
Trains	296
Transporters	296
Mystery Heads	302
Ads and Programs	303
The Crowd Roars	309
Index	311

Preface

I've been an auto racing nut forever. It all started at age six, in 1930, when my folks took me to a race at San Jose Speedway in California. I remember rooting for a certain driver. When his car had trouble and he fell out of the race, I cried. I like to think I've matured since then.

As a kid, growing up in San Francisco, I saw the big cars, roadsters, stock cars and midgets run at several Bay area tracks. Quarter midgets and the like did not exist then, so the only actual racing I did was in the gravity-powered Soap Box Derby cars. World War II interrupted any thoughts I had of becoming a race driver, and I saw service in Europe as a combat infantryman.

After the war it was college, and it wasn't until 1948 that I converted my street hot rod into a track roadster. This was a Model A, heavy as a boat anchor, with a too small Ford V-8 engine. It was totally uncompetitive but somehow I learned to drive a race car.

Later on, there were faster track roadsters. By 1950 the roadsters were fading out, so it was on to sprint cars. In 1951 my brother, Les, and I built a sprinter that was, in some ways, well ahead of its time—it had a space tube frame. Despite a mid-season flip at

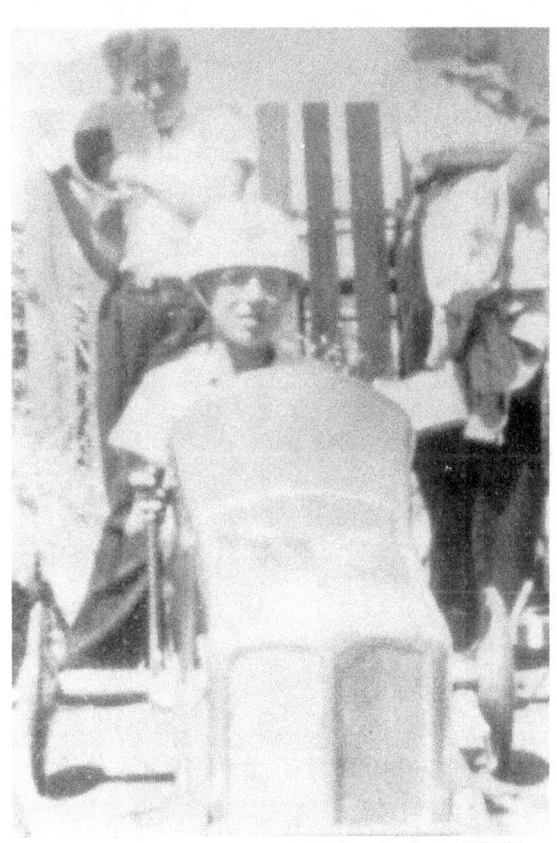

1938, San Francisco. My first race car—a soap box derby (Walter Radbruch photograph).

Top: 1951—Calistoga, California. Me in the Don and Les Radbruch tube-frame Merc (Les Radbruch photograph). *Bottom:* 1996—Bellville, Kansas. It's a thrill to sit in the Lou Kleinau Winfield Rocker Arm car (Dave Imrie photograph).

Calistoga, this car carried me to the 1951 American Racing Association (ARA) championship.

The ARA was certainly not big time, but what the heck, a championship is a championship. I continued with the sprints, with some stock cars and hardtops mixed in, for a couple of years until I figured out that this sort of thing was dangerous. From 1954 to 1967 I mostly confined my racing to the Bay Cities Racing Association (BCRA) indoor midgets at Oakland. I did venture outdoors in sporty cars to tracks like Laguna Seca. I had a lot of fun racing, survived seven times upside down in those pre-roll cage days, and banked payoffs that ranged from $1.34 to $670.

My interest in racing history and writing extends back almost forever. As a kid I wrote a few articles on the San Francisco Motordrome midgets for *Illustrated Speedway News*. In the mid–1950s I wrote several historical articles for *Speed Age*. At that point I became deeply involved with my job as a soil engineer, and it wasn't until the mid–1980s that I started chasing racing history again. This time it was for Ken Breslauer's *Auto Racing Memories*. One thing led to another, and I wound up interested in track roadster racing history. From this came my first book, *Roaring Roadsters*, published in 1994. A second hot rod book followed and *Roaring Roadsters 2* was published only recently. Racing history research, writing and photo work now keep me busy nearly full time. This includes articles for Phyllis Devine's *The Alternate* and Charlie Yapp's *Secrets Magazine*.

This book focuses on the dirt track racing phenomenon of the 1920s and the 1930s, when there was racing on a thousand dirt tracks in the United States and Canada. Most of it was small-time racing with small purses and minimal publicity. If there was any record of the races it was in small-town newspapers—a thousand of them. Needless to say, this sort of thing is a bit difficult to research.

Some fine books have been written on '20s and '30s racing. Some authors limited their research to a specific track—usually a well-known speedway. A few books have been written about a more general area, but these pick up on maybe 10 percent of what went on. This book is an attempt to make a dent in the missing 90 percent.

I don't claim to have collected everything that happened in dirt track racing between the two World Wars. Additional research could have been done on innumerable items. The book could have been a thousand pages long, but I don't think the publisher would want to pay the printing bill, and I don't have 50 more years to spend writing such a monster. I've concentrated on material that should be mostly new to the reader, since it has not been covered in other racing books. In other words, material that has been all but forgotten.

Despite being a bit over 39 years old I still have not outgrown race cars. I drive vintage midgets and sprinters with the Pacific Northwest-based Golden Wheels group at every opportunity. Did I say that I thought I'd matured from that first race in San Jose? Maybe I haven't!

About the Photographs

Relatively few photographs in this book were taken by professional photographers. Few professionals were taking photographs of dirt track racing in the 1920s

Preface

and 1930s, especially at the less well known tracks that existed all around the country.

Many of the photographs in this book were taken by amateurs—perhaps members of the racers' families. They used cameras that were primitive by today's standards. Available shutter speeds were slow and telephoto lenses did not exist. Action photos were difficult to take and hence are fairly rare—I wish there were more in these pages. On the plus side, most of the old cameras took large negatives so that photos for the book did not need extreme enlargement. Those old cameras must have had very good lenses as most photos are clear and sharp.

Photos for this book were borrowed from a couple of hundred different sources. I've credited the person who lent me each photograph or the collection from which a photo came. Every attempt has been made to credit the photographer, but in most cases this was not possible.

Most information about the photos came from what was written on the back of the originals. All too often this would be more than a bit cryptic: something like, "All of us at the track."

Thanks to all who lent me the photographs. Without you this book would not exist!

Comments, additional information (and even corrections!) regarding this book are welcome at 450 Road 39G, Sagle ID 83860. E-mail is *radbruch@sandpoint.net*.

Don Radbruch

Introduction
Big Cars, Outlaws, and Midgets

This is the story of the real beginnings of automobile racing pretty much as we know it today. Starting around 1919, the "little guy" could build or buy a race car and go racing. Prior to that year, most automobile racing involved expensive machines and teams financed by the manufacturers. These teams toured the country, and most of the races were in large cities. The vast majority of Americans never saw an auto race.

World War I changed all this. When Johnny came marching home he'd seen a chunk of the world. Maybe Johnny was restless and wanted excitement. Maybe he was inspired by Henry's wonderful Model T which could so easily be converted to a race car. Johnny and his Model T went racing at the local fairgrounds, and a new era began.

Big Cars

What Johnny developed was what would come to be called, in the 1930s, a "big car," and, a few decades later, a sprint car. Model T Fords were bound to be a favorite. They were inexpensive, and the little car's engine gave a surprising turn of speed to a lightweight racer. Some cars—"bobtails"—had no rear body at all; otherwise, what bodywork there was behind the driver's seat usually tapered to a pointed tail. By the 1930s, those early crude attempts at streamlining evolved into some really handsome designs.

Since sitting on top of a race car's gas tank wasn't such a good idea, the T's under-the-front-seat tank was usually replaced by one fastened behind a deep bucket seat. The seat's sides kept the driver in place. Seat belts didn't come into common use for many years. Roll bars were unheard of. Helmets? No way! A few drivers opted for a leather helmet, but bare heads or a cloth cap and goggles were the norm.

It didn't take long for men used to tinkering to decide that the stock Ford or

Chevy or whatever could use a little "improving." The speed-equipment industry was born. Race cars began to be built out of pieces—frame rails from one make, front axle and suspension from another, maybe an engine from a third.

The Ford engine—T, A, or B—remained the basis of the average race car. Most early engines, including Ford, had the valves in the block rather than in the head (upside-down, by modern standards). While the "flathead" engines could be modified into potent racing engines, a better solution was to cast an entirely new head for the engine that would contain overhead valves. A few racers designed and built their own overhead-valve units, but heads were available from dozens of manufacturers at reasonable prices. A very few even devised an overhead-cam setup. One of the most popular overhead-valve conversions was the Frontenac ("Fronty"), developed by Arthur Chevrolet. Fronty Fords became a mainstay of pre-World War II racing. By the late '20s, Chevrolet's company—not the same as the passenger-car maker—and others would sell you a ready-to-go race car. Rajo conversions for the Model T were also popular.

If a driver had money—or was good enough to attract a car owner or sponsor who had money—he might drive a Duesenberg or a Miller. Before the magnificent Model Js became the favorites of movie stars and millionaires, Duesenberg built potent race cars, including four Indianapolis 500 winners. Harry Miller built some of the most successful American racing cars of the 1920s and 1930s. Many of his cars were lovely to look at, with a distinctive elegantly shaped radiator grille. Miller and Duesenberg engines also found their way into some "specials." The era also saw the birth of the Offenhauser engine—the fabled "Offy" that powered everything from midgets to Indy 500 winners right up to the 1970s.

Outlaws

Big car racing was ruled with an iron hand by the American Automobile Association. Before surrendering control to the United States Auto Club (USAC) in 1955, the AAA was the governing body of major auto racing in the United States. AAA representatives served as "zone supervisors" in various parts of the country. The group was dedicated and well-meaning, and the men even paid most of their own expenses while doing their job, but some of them were also a bit pompous and totally inflexible. As early as 1916 the AAA began punishing drivers who ran in non–AAA sanctioned events. It called them "outlaws."

For the top drivers the AAA was a good deal. The races were well officiated, and not only were the purses guaranteed but the money had to be in the hands of the AAA official before the race started. It was a businesslike arrangement, and the top drivers could race often enough to make a good living. For the also-rans on the AAA circuits, it was not such a good deal. They didn't have steady rides, and some could not afford to travel around the country to the AAA races. These men had to take their chances in local events run, perhaps, by fly-by-night, less-than-honest promoters. Many of the so-called "outlaw" groups, however, were good outfits to race for. The International Motor Contest Association (IMCA), the Central States Racing Association (CSRA), and a dozen other such organizations were well run, and the likelihood of the drivers' being cheated was small. Beyond these groups was racing that would have to be called "outlaw outlaw"—here things could get a bit rough.

When a AAA driver strayed from the flock he faced a suspension and a stiff fine. He was forbidden to compete in AAA races until the fine was paid. For severe violations the driver could receive a lifetime ban; Barney Oldfield collected several of these. Drivers would often run outlaw races under phony names, but this seldom concealed their identity. Some of the fines were big numbers for the times—as much as $500 or $1,000. Whether fines this large were ever paid is not known. Data from official AAA records of West Coast races in the early 1930s provide some interesting information. Drivers and owners hit with fines would make payments of five or ten dollars and apparently be permitted to race in a given event. If a banned driver showed up with a good AAA car at a race where the field was a bit short, some deals were probably made. Here are excerpts from a 1935 AAA list of fines:

Pacific Coast Fines
August 22, 1935

Axel, Lloyd	Driver	$100	Paid $25.00	
Balmer, Everett	Driver	$200	Paid $10.00	Outlaw again
Cole, Hal	Driver	$100	Paid $17.50	
Durant, Louis	Driver	$100	Paid $5.00	
Haddad, Ed	Driver	$100	Paid $5.00	
Kerbs, L.E.	Owner	$25	Paid $10.00	Outlaw again
Martinson, Art	Driver	$250	Paid $60.00	Outlaw again
Mansell, Earl	Driver	$100		Outlaw again
McGurk, Frank	Driver	$100	Paid $6.00	
Roberts, Floyd	Driver	$300	Paid $170.00	
Taylor, Jack	Owner	$100	Paid $27.00	Outlaw again

Midgets

When the first midgets rolled out onto an improvised track at Hughes Stadium in Sacramento, California, on June 4, 1933, few people realized that a huge change in racing was about to take place. Here was a totally different class of race car that would soon challenge the well-established full-sized race cars all over the country. It took a while for the midgets to show the speed to threaten the soon-to-be-called "big cars," but in a few short years they had a major share of the racing fans' dollars.

Midget racing spread across the nation like wildfire, and by 1936 there were hundreds of midget speedways. These little cars could race in a baseball park, around a football field, or on a short track carved out of the infield of the county fair half-miler. It wasn't long before special speedways were build for the midgets—tracks that were not suited to the big cars. Even though most of the midget racing was at night, the big cars found that they were hurting at the box office on Sunday. The popularity of midget racing was a factor in the demise of tracks like Legion Ascot Speedway.

At first, relatively few big car drivers tried driving midgets. Perhaps they considered them toys, or beneath their abilities as race drivers. They were truly "midget," with a wheelbase of barely more than six feet. At first their builders used motorcycle or outboard motor engines, or a four- or six-cylinder engine cut in half. Soon Offenhauser came out with a midget engine, and ultimately the 60 H.P. Ford V-8 became popular. The drivers of those early midgets were almost exclusively newcomers to a new sport. As the midgets evolved into better machines, and as the purses rose, many big car drivers put aside their doubts and drove midgets at every opportunity.

The biggest effect on the fortunes of the big cars was near the big cities where most of the midget tracks were located—there was midget racing nearly every night. Out in the hinterlands it wasn't quite so bad, but even here the midgets were a thorn in the side of the big cars. Many of the county fairs that had traditionally run the big cars switched to the midgets. Today big car (sprint car) racing is healthy, but it shares the fans' interest with the midgets—to say nothing of who knows how many classes of stock cars. The big cars never fully recovered from the onslaught of the midgets; their monopoly ended on June 4, 1933.

1

Pacific Coast
Washington, Oregon, California

Washington first saw auto racing at Spokane in 1909 at the Interstate Fairgrounds. Surprisingly, the promoters managed to scrape up enough Pacific Northwest cars to put on a show. Tacoma had racing starting in 1914 on a two-mile dirt oval—this track was later replaced with the better known board speedway. In Seattle a AAA race was scheduled in 1914 at the Seattle Motor Speedway but might not

Pop Evans is shown at a Southern California track with his very fast Flathead Model T. Evans was active as a driver and car owner from about 1917 until the 1940s. He was also the track maintenance man at Legion Ascot and Oakland Speedways (Johnny Klann collection).

have taken place. Walla Walla did have a race on May 30, 1917. In the 1920s there was racing at Vancouver, across the Columbia River from Portland, and at Centralia. In 1926 the first events were held on the one-and-one-eighth-mile horse track at Yakima and this racing went on until after World War II. Silver Lake Speedway at Everett hosted races beginning in 1927 and the track was active until the late 1930s, with a couple of races after the war. Seattle had racing in 1931 and 1932 at the downtown Seattle Municipal Stadium oval. In 1936 Aurora Speedway opened north of town to replace the nearby, short-lived Olympic View Speedway. This five-eighths-mile banked oval saw lots of action until 1942. While 1930s racing in Washington is fairly well docu-

Left: Omar Toft has some problems with his Duesenberg. It is believed that this photograph was taken at Ascot Park in about 1919 (Tom Saal collection). *Bottom:* An unknown driver and his riding mechanic at Los Banos, California in 1920 (Milliken Museum).

mented there is little information for the 1920s, and additional race tracks no doubt existed in that decade. The known 1920s racing in Washington was on the beaches in the southwest corner of the sate in 1923 and at Elma in 1924.

In Oregon, Portland had street racing as early as 1909 but the first oval track race was probably at Medford in 1913. This was the only known racing in Oregon until about 1920 when racing began at Portland Speedway—probably at the same location on Union Avenue where Portland Speedway operated until 2001. This track was once known as Rankin Field and was paved in about 1937. Portland also had racing at the Gresham Speedbowl from 1928 to 1937 and at the Base Line Speedbowl in 1934—this might have been a re-named Gresham. Medord had AAA races complete with Ralph De Palma in 1924 and 1925. The Oregon State Fairgrounds in Salem had races on a mile oval in about 1927 and 1929 and then, in the 1930s, on a half-mile track. In the 1930s there were races at Grants Pass, Medford, McMinnville, and Tillamook. In about 1930 there was racing east of the Cascades at Klamath Falls and maybe at Bend.

California had racing on over 50 tracks prior to World War II. Northern California first saw racing on November 4, 1904, at the Ingleside track in San Francisco. The one-mile oval also held races in 1904, and races were scheduled for 1906 but canceled because of the earthquake. Strangely enough this track still

Harry Saunders of Santa Maria sends us this photo of one of the "hot irons" of 1921. We are not sure, but think the owner and driver is Monty Houck of Lompoc, who was one of the "high-rolling" castor burners of that day.

Top: This photograph is from a 1934 issue of *Coast Auto Racing*. Monte Houck won a lot of races in this Model T. Most were road or street races in Central California but this is an oval track race—maybe in Santa Maria (Bob Garner collection). *Bottom:* Rajo Jack drove this neat looking bobtail in early 1920s races in Oregon and Washington. Note the unusual quarter elliptical front springs. The engine is a T with a Rajo Overhead Valve Head (Herman Giles collection).

No tail to put the number on? No problem—put it on the driver. Rajo Jack at Portland in 1923. Despite lots of steel this car was hundreds of pounds lighter than today's sprint cars (Herman Giles collection).

"exists" as houses were built around it. It became a street and still shows up as an oval in the normal rectangular street pattern of the area. There were races at several other Northern California locations prior to 1910, but apparently, there was no further racing until the 1920s. (The racing at the 1915 San Francisco World's Fair was road racing.) In the 1920s occasional races were held at Pleasanton, Stockton, Petaluma, Santa Rosa and Salinas. The Tanforan horse track, a few miles south of San Francisco, had a couple of AAA races in 1924 and 1925. In 1923 San Jose Speedway opened and operated with varying degrees of success until 1939. In 1931 the high-banked one-mile Oakland Speedway opened its doors. A few years later a half-mile flat oval was built in the infield and both tracks ran until 1941. During the 1930s races were held at the Eastside Track in San Jose, Watsonville, and Willits. The now-famed Calistoga half-miler hosted a few big car races, as well as the roadsters, from 1937 until 1941.

Central California's first auto races were held in Fresno on October 10, 1904, and racing continued on the mile track until about 1916. In Bakersfield there was racing from 1913 to about 1918 on a mile track at the old Kern County Fairgrounds. (In 1913 Barney Oldfield set one of his many "World Records" at this track). Occasional AAA races were held on this oval in the 1920s and early 1930s—at some time during this period the track was known as the Derkum Dirt Track. In 1931 and 1932 a half-mile track was constructed at the same site for races with outlaw cars and drivers. Other racing from the 1920s until World War II was at Chowchilla, Los Banos, Goshen and Newhall. Over on the Central California coast, Santa Maria had fairgrounds racing from 1919 to 1941. Pismo Beach had an oval track in 1919 and, in later years, racing around barrels on the beach. San Luis Obispo had racing from 1919 to 1941, and in the early years this was AAA-sanctioned with top-flight drivers on hand.

Opposite top: Ed Winfield at San Luis Obispo, California, in the early 1920s. The car is a Flathead T with a strange-looking front suspension. Until he turned to cam grinding and engine building, Winfield was a fine driver (Doug Boyd collection from Johnny Klann). *Bottom:* Fred Wallace is shown at San Jose in 1924. Wallace was a winner in California races, but—like so many drivers of the era—very little is known about his racing career. Note the unusually high position of the exhaust headers—what is the engine type? (Bob Rushing collection).

1. *Pacific Coast* (WA, OR, CA)

Southern California had racing at 14 locations during the years prior to World War I. Of these, five were dirt ovals. The first racing was at Agricultural Park in Los Angeles in 1903. The original Ascot was built in 1904 as a horse track and exhibition runs by autos might have taken place as early as 1908. Horse racing was banned in 1910, and at some point the track was improved for auto racing, with occasional events being held until 1919. It is possible that the popular Beverly Hills Board Track (1920–1924) discouraged the development of dirt tracks; the next known racing on the dirt was in 1923 at the Riverside Fairgrounds. In 1924 the five-eighths-mile oiled dirt Ascot Speedway was built. This would become known as the Legion Ascot Speedway—one of the most famous (infamous?) tracks in racing history. Culver City had a one-mile dirt track that ran for several years before the board track was built in late 1924. Racing is known to have started at Banning on a half-mile track in 1926, but there might have been an earlier one-mile oval at the same location. Other Los Angeles–area racing in the 1920s was at Ventura, and about 1930 at Redlands. Legion Ascot closed in 1936 but by the next year there was another "Ascot Speedway" on the scene. This track was first known as Southern Speedway and then as Southern Ascot, but was usually referred to as "South Gate" from its location. This speedway, a flat half-mile paved oval, ran from 1937 until 1942.

Of interest in the Los Angeles area is Mines Field. This was a "B" shaped dirt

The field gets ready to go on the one-mile San Luis Obispo oval in 1923—or perhaps earlier. These are local, or West Coast, cars, and a few of them carry riding mechanics (Parsons collection).

Top: Leigh Green in action at Culver City in 1924. The Culver City board track was constructed on this site later that year and operated until 1927. A few races were held on the dirt after the board track was torn down, but nails from the boards were a problem (Sowle collection; photograph by Wilson). *Bottom:* Ralph DePalma at San Luis Obispo in about 1923. This was either a AAA event or one sanctioned by the Western Racing Association. It is a safe bet that DePalma took home lots of money (Parsons collection).

Top: Jerry Wonderlick at San Jose for a AAA race. Wonderlick took part in five Indy 500s and had 42 starts on the boards (Bob Rushing collection). *Bottom:* A fine 1923 action shot at San Luis Obispo. Most cameras of the day did not have fast shutter speeds, so the photographer had to film action at an angle. Here the photographer obviously risks his life by standing on the outside of the turn. Adolph Guisti leads Fred Luelling (Parson collection).

Top: Carl Mikkelsen at the wheel of his front-wheel-drive T at Ascot in 1924. Mikkelsen was a talented machinist and designer and usually left the driving to others. His FWD setup ran for several years with no problems; at one point, Mikkelsen installed a conventional rear end and had four-wheel drive (Frank Mikkelsen collection). *Bottom:* Ed Winfield in his Kant Score Special in about 1924. Later on, Winfield took this Flathead T out on the Culver City boards and ran a lap at a reported 110 MPH (Johnny Klann collection).

track that was a combination of an oval and a road-race circuit. In 1934 a AAA stock car and an Indy car race were run here; in 1936 the American Racing Association sanctioned a stock car race and a less-than-successful big car event. Mines Field is now the site of the Los Angeles International Airport.

Further south, San Diego had racing that started on a dirt oval in 1913—this might have been beach racing. Silvergate Speedway operated from 1932 to 1936. This was a five-eighths-mile track located near the present site of Sea World. Neil's Sportsman Park was another five-eighths-miler that ran briefly in 1932–33.

Top left: Fred Luelling was thrown clear of this San Jose crash and had only minor injuries. Oldtimer Johnny Klann remembers, "In those flimsy cars you were better off being thrown out." He does add the proviso, "unless you landed on your head!" (Parsons collection). *Top right:* Speed Hinkley drove this nice looking T bobtail at Banning, California, in the mid–1920s. Note that the frame is reinforced with wood! (Levrett collection). *Bottom:* E.J. Lucke, the Banning Ford dealer, points out the "snubbers" on his eight-valve Rajo T. Shock technology was a bit primitive in 1926 (Toprahanian collection).

Top: Herb Hipnett is shown at Banning in Herb Stang's 490 Chevy. These 167-cubic-inch four-cylinder engines with an Oldsmobile three-port head would hold their own against the Model T's (Toprahanian collection). *Bottom:* The location is uncertain, maybe Banning, but Emmet Larson is all smiles after he has won a nice trophy (Toprahanian collection; photograph by Donaldson).

Top: There is a nice crowd on hand as the field gets ready for the start at Banning. Racing at this Southern California city went on from 1926 to 1929—some of the races were under AAA sanction (Toprahanian collection; photograph by Donaldson). *Bottom:* Banning in 1926. No dust, but the smoke makes it tough for the backmarkers to see. Car number 22, in the pits, is Ted Simpson's huge Chrysler Eight (Toprahanian collection).

Left: Mel Kenealy drove Harry Hooker's T at Banning and other California tracks. The Hooker T had a DOHC Model T engine with a steel billet crankshaft that reportedly cost $500. The engine stayed together at 5500 RPM! There are reports that Harry Miller built the DOHC unit for Hooker's Model T. *Above:* Bill Spence nearly bounces out of the Hooker T at Banning. This photograph graphically illustrates just how dangerous the bobtails were. Spence survived these machines only to die at Indianapolis in 1929 (Above photographs—Johnny Klann collection). *Below:* Babe Stapp was another of Harry Hooker's drivers—was Hooker hard to get along with? Stapp ran at Indy from 1927 to 1940; after World War II, he promoted races (Sowie collection).

Top: Here are some well-known racing people. Pop Evans was a long-time West Coast personality. Art Sparks of Indy fame needs no introduction. Paul Fromm owned Legion Ascot cars driven by Rex Mays. That is Sherman Quick in the car. *Bottom:* Johnny Klann at Pismo Beach in Central California in 1934. Straightaway speed trials were held, and then the cars raced around barrels placed a half-mile apart on the beach. Klann remembers that his Fronty was clocked at 86 MPH on a soggy beach (Both photographs—Johnny Klann collection).

Top: Great racing action, possibly at Tri-Cities Speedway in San Bernardino, California, in 1932. Tex Peterson is in the foreground in Jack Taylor's SO Fronty with Essex driver Floyd Roberts on the outside (Dick Downes collection). *Middle:* Curley Mills in the Pop Evans Flathead Model A at Pismo Beach. Mills soon switched to the midgets and was the driver of the original "Mighty Midget"—the first Offy. He suffered fatal injures at the Madison Square Garden Bowl in New York in 1936 (Johnny Klann collection). *Bottom:* Billy Arnold at Oakland in about 1932. Arnold started racing in the Chicago area and first appeared at Indy in 1928. He won the 500 in 1930, but crashed out of competition in both 1931 and 1932 (George Sowle collection).

Top: Chris Vest suffered serious burns before he was able to get out of this car. The incident took place in one of the first races at Oakland Speedway (George Sowle collection; photograph by Ted Wilson). *Bottom:* Harry Gentry suffered fatal injuries in this 1935 crash at Silvergate Speedway in San Diego. Gentry had been married on the previous day (Johnny Klann collection).

Top: Gus Schrader made a rare California visit and drove Barney Klaupher's car at San Jose in 1931. Reports are that he finished second in the main event to Babe Stapp. Other sources indicate that Schrader's West Coast invasion was less than successful—especially at Legion Ascot (Don Radbruch collection). *Bottom:* A pit scene at San Jose in the early 1930s. Odds are it is a AAA event as there is a large crowd on hand (Chini collection).

Top: Mario Branchero in about 1935. Branchero drove both roadsters and big cars under the rather uncomplimentary alias of "Fat Mario." He was a better-than-average driver on Northern California tracks (Don Radbruch collection). *Middle:* A typical San Jose car around 1932. The photograph was taken by Jack Carmody, who later announced races in the Bay Area. Carmody took a lot of photographs like this with no identification (Chini collection). *Bottom:* Duane Carter gets a trophy at an unknown racetrack in about 1936. The trophy girl is Mrs. Fred (Mabel) Agabashian. Carter was just getting started on a road that led to Indy and a AAA sprint car championship (Chini collection; photograph by Carmody).

Top: Bayliss Levrett in a nice looking big car at San Jose—probably in August of 1939. Levrett had a long career as a driver. *Bottom:* Silvergate Speedway in San Diego was a fine racing facility and held races from 1932 to 1936. It is now the site of Sea World. (Both photographs—Levrett collection)

Top: Rajo Jack in the Pop Evans Flathead A at Silvergate Speedway in San Diego—1934. That's Pop Evans at the right. This car was a longtime fixture of California racing; the author remembers racing against it as late as 1952 (Herman Giles collection). *Middle:* Curley Mills at Silvergate in 1934. This Walter Church car was a consistent winner at the San Diego five-eighths-mile oval. Note that Mills wears a football helmet—an improvement over the normal cloth helmet. *Bottom:* Bayliss Levrett in #1 takes the lead from Howard Cox on the last turn of a 75-lapper at Silvergate. (Middle and bottom photographs—Levrett collection)

Top: Earl Mansell gets a nice trophy at Silvergate. Blessed with fine weather, this track could operate nearly 12 months a year and did so for several years. Silvergate also ran a few stock car races—somewhat of a rarity in those days. *Bottom:* This is Tri-Cities Speedway near San Bernardino, California. A bit of dust but not bad for the times (Both photographs—Levrett collection).

Above: Frank Wearne leads Jimmy Wilburn around the Rankin Track (paved soon after) at Portland in 1936. *Left:* Swede Lindskog began his career in the Pacific Northwest big cars and midgets. He soon moved to Southern California and starred in the Gilmore Stadium midgets until his death at that track in 1946 (McMurtry collection). *Below:* The lineup at Yakima, Washington, in about 1936. Mel Kenealy is in the #1 Roach Miller. The Yakima track was 1⅛-mile oval—fast, dusty, and dangerous (Top and bottom photographs—Eckert collection from Pike Green).

Top: Yakima in 1934. The track was no doubt built for horses but was exclusively used for auto racing from the 1930s to the 1950s. Those fences were deadly but had to be ignored. *Bottom:* Bill Strong at Yakima in 1934. The Gilmore Oil Company was a big booster of racing in the 1930s and sponsored cars on the West Coast as well as at Indy (Both photographs—Eckert collection from Pike Green).

Top: Mario Bianchi starred in Pacific Northwest racing from the early 1920s until the late 1930s. This very-nice-looking Miller would be hard to beat at Yakima. *Middle:* This is probably Woody Woodford at Yakima. He was another of the Legion Ascot drivers who migrated north when that track closed (Both photographs—Eckert collection from Pike Green). *Bottom:* Mel Kenealy at Yakima in 1936. Kenealy was AAA Pacific Southwest Champion in 1929 and starred at Legion Ascot in the early 1930s. He was one of several drivers who apparently moved to Oregon or Washington when Ascot was closed (McMurtry collection).

Top: Bill Strong tangled with the fence at Yakima. Odds are Strong got lost in the dust. *Bottom:* Del Valentine was one of the most popular drivers in Oregon and Washington. He died in a 1936 crash at Yakima (Both photographs—Eckert collection from Pike Green).

Top left: An unidentified driver in a bobtail at Yakima in 1933. Can you imagine how brave this man had to be to drive this car on that track? *Top right:* This might have been one of the last bobtail cars to race in the United States—1934 at Yakima. That is not a Ford V-8—perhaps a LaSalle or Cadillac? *Bottom:* Joe Williamson was one of the few semi-professional photographers in the Pacific Northwest. Odds are he charged a dime for a four-by-five and a quarter for an 8-by-10 print. This is Yakima (Above photographs—Eckert collection from Pike Green).

Top: Johnny McDowell is another of the nationally famous racers who got his start in the Pacific Northwest. Here he is at the Aurora Speedbowl near Seattle in 1936. McDowell took this car to the Midwest later that year (Sweigert collection). *Middle:* State-of-the-art safety equipment in 1936. Jimmy Wilburn at Silverlake Speedway near Everett, Washington. Yes—that is a cut-down fireman's helmet! *Bottom:* Lew McMurtry at Silverlake in about 1936. McMurtry was a winner in Oregon, Washington and British Columbia races. He had more than his share of crashes but somehow survived (Middle and bottom photographs—Eckert collection from Pike Green).

Top: This is either Yakima or Gresham Speedway near Portland. Racers knocked down a lot of fences at both places. *Bottom:* Matt Milos was fatally injured in this July 1934 crash at Gresham Speedway. Beyond the wooden fences was the additional hazard of the trees. (Both photographs—Eckert collection from Pike Green)

Top: Adolph Dans was one of the drivers of the Neeley Burkitt Chrome Miller. Here he is shown after a 100-lap victory at Portland in 1938. Dans kept busy with both the big cars and the midgets (Bill Hill collection). *Middle:* Claude Walling in the Mel Anthony car in 1939. Walling was just getting started in racing and most of his career took place after World War II (Carmel Sandy collection). *Bottom:* Oakland Speedway in 1933, and a big crowd is on hand for the AAA-sanctioned races. When the presentation was first class, Bay Area fans turned out at Oakland in goodly numbers (Don Radbruch collection).

Top: Bob Scovell in 1932. Scovell usually raced in the Pacific Northwest but he also competed at Legion Ascot. After World War II Scovell and his wife, Vi, were the main forces behind big car racing in Oregon and Washington. *Bottom:* Stan Mahony somehow survived this 1938 crash at Portland's Rankin Track (Both photographs—McMurtry collection).

Top: Les Anderson at Seattle's Aurora Speedway in 1937. Anderson was a winner in Oregon and Washington, and after World War II made it to Indy. He drove his own Offy to an 11th place finish in 1947, and was out with mechanical problems in 1948. He died in a Portland big car crash on July 10, 1949 (McMurtry collection). *Botttom:* Ernie Criss tangles with the fence at Oakland in 1935. Criss campaigned California big cars and midgets for many years; while not a big winner, he was a better-than-average driver (Sowle collection).

Top: Walt Davis calmly strolls away from his burning race car at Oakland in 1939. Davis had the same thing happen the previous year at Oakland. Do you get used to having your race car burn up? *Bottom:* Action on Oakland's flat half-miler in about 1937. Duane Carter spins out and collects the #18 of "Fat Mario" Branchero, who wound up flipping with only minor hurts. Carter got his start in Northern California racing and moved on to national prominence (Both photographs—George Sowle collection).

Top: Bill Johnson at Oakland Speedway in 1938. The Chevy Four appears to have the stock one port head rather than the normal Olds three-porter. Johnson died while practicing for the 1940 Oakland 500 (Chick Lasteri collection). *Bottom:* Tex Peterson is shown with owner Gil Pearson in 1939. Peterson did most of his racing in California, but also made several trips to run with the IMCA in the Midwest (Ray Hiatt collection).

Left: Wally Schock was one of the leading drivers on the Pacific Coast and won the American Racing Association championship in 1939 and 1940. Serious injuries in World War II battle action prevented his return to racing after the conflict (Loren Kreck collection). *Right:* Wally Schock shows how a race driver should look after a tough dirt-track event. This is Oakland in 1941 (Don Radbruch photograph).

The Other Aggie

To most racing fans in the United States, "Aggie" is J.C. Agajanian, the well-known car owner and race promoter. To northern Californians "Aggie" is also Fred Agabashian—race driver par excellence.

Freddy Agabashian's racing career spanned three decades as he racked up victories in the big cars, midgets and stock cars. He began racing in the roadsters at San Jose in 1934, and promptly suffered serious injuries in a crash. From the roadsters Agabashian moved on to the big cars, and was the first American Racing Association champion in 1936. Freddy's first love was really the midgets and he won a 1937 Northern California championship as well as racking up seven straight wins at the San Francisco Motordrome. He continued to drive the big cars and found time to win a couple of long distance stock car races at the Oakland Speedway.

Fred Agabashian waits for the start of a race at Oakland Speedway in about 1938—that's car owner Jack Stevens at the right. The car is the beautiful DOHC Cragar Occidental Chrome Special (Ray Hiatt collection).

After World War II Agabashian starred in the rough and tumble Bay Cities Racing Association (BCRA) and was a three-time champion. His first Indy experience was in 1946 when he drove the Ross Page Offy to a ninth place finish. Agabashian drove at Indy until 1958, with his best finish a fourth in 1953—he won the pole in the Cummins Diesel in 1952.

"Aggie" was one of the few drivers of his caliber that held down a full-time job while racing; hence, except for Indy, he stuck pretty close to home. He made only a few starts in AAA Champ car racing on the dirt, but one of these was a victory in the 1949 Sacramento hundred-miler. Oddly enough he was driving for the other "Aggie."

Ascot

There were three Ascot Speedways in Los Angeles. Of these, Legion Ascot is certainly the most famous—or, perhaps, infamous. The latest Ascot closed in 1996. The first Ascot has been all but forgotten.

There is no need to attempt to differentiate the three Ascots by location in Los

Angeles—to most of us, that city is a huge blob that covers most of Southern California. The first Ascot was a one-mile oval built for horse racing in 1904 and called Ascot Park after the famous English track. The horses ran there until 1910 when betting on horses became illegal in California.

It appears that there were auto races, or at least exhibitions, at Ascot as early as 1908. These were dusty events as horse owners forbid the use of water, oil or other surface preparation. The track surface was completely oiled in 1916 and, thereafter, auto races were held on a regular basis. At this point it might have been called Ascot Speedway. Unfortunately very little information on these races is available. Some of the events must have been under AAA sanction as drivers like Eddie Hearne and Eddie Rickenbacker competed at Ascot.

Depending on which source of information is used, Ascot was swallowed up by urban development in either 1919 or 1920, although there is a chance that an IMCA event was held there in 1922. The races were so successful that a new race track was built in Los Angeles shortly after the demise of the original Ascot. Built in 1924, this was called the New Ascot Speedway—in a few years it would become Legion Ascot.

No attempt will be made to cover the history of Legion Ascot in detail in these pages. John Lucero has done an excellent job of this in his book, *Legion Ascot Speedway*.

Goshen, 1934

A number of races were held in this Central California town during the 1930s. Both the big cars and the roadsters raced, but for the most part the results have long since been forgotten. Thanks to Johnny Klann of La Canada, California, we have data on a 1934 Goshen event.

The big crowd at Goshen is shown in the background as Pierre Bertrand gets ready to race his Flathead Model A. Bertrand quit racing after a bad spill at Legion Ascot and became a noted cam grinder (Johnny Klann collection).

The race was well promoted (except for one minor detail) and attracted a large crowd and good field of cars and drivers. In the starting lineup were drivers like Floyd Roberts, who would win the 1938 Indy 500, Frank Wearne and Curly Mills. No doubt Goshen was dusty in the summer heat of the San Joaquin Valley but it was a

Top: Johnny Klann is shown in the Terry Fronty at Goshen. Klann drove roadsters and big cars in the early to mid–1930s before retiring because of family responsibilities. He is now one of the most respected racing historians in the country. *Bottom:* This is how race drivers are supposed to look after a race! Left to right are fourth-place finisher Norman Muir, winner Floyd Roberts and third-place Johnny Klann. Muir looks remarkably clean—was he a *distant* fourth? (Both photographs—Johnny Klann collection).

fine show and everybody had a good time. For Johnny Klann it was his best career finish as he drove the I. B. Terry SO Fronty and wound up third in the feature event.

The "minor detail" surfaced when it came time for the payoff. It seems the promoter had left a few unpaid bills behind after a previous Goshen race, and it was the local sheriff who collected the lion's share of the purse—all of it! The racers passed the hat among the crowd, so there was a payoff of sorts. Winner Floyd Roberts received $38, second place Frank Wearne $18, and Johnny Klann got all of $8 for his efforts that day. This was money paid to the car owners—drivers usually got one-third back then. In the photo below Johnny Klann looks very happy for just having raced for something like $2.67!

Oakland—500 Miles on the Dirt

History has done an excellent job of forgetting the Oakland 500-mile races. Today these long races are a dime a dozen, but prior to World War II 500-mile races were held only at Indy, in 1915 at Chicago and Minneapolis, and at Oakland Speedway.

Oakland Speedway was a banked one-mile oval that was built in 1931. Subject

Top: Bud Rose (Harry Elsele) was the winner of the first Oakland 500 in 1938. Car owner Gil Pearson, is at the left. Do you recognize the man on the right? Correct—that's J. C. Agajanian (Ray Hiatt collection). *Bottom:* A nearly full house is on hand for the start of the 1940 Oakland 500. Hal Cole jumped into the lead and pretty well dominated the long race. Although the race advertised 33 starters, the best promoter Charlie Curryer could do in the four races was around 30 (Chini collection).

to the whims of the publicists Oakland was either "The World's Fastest Mile Track" or "The World's Fastest Dirt Track." No doubt it was fast. Al Gordon went 106.32 MPH at Oakland in 1933—it wasn't until 1948 that Tony Bettenhausen went a bit faster on a mile track at Langhorne. The surface at Oakland was heavily oiled dirt. The racing groove was much like pavement except that it tended to break up during a long race—outside the groove it was loose dirt.

In the early and mid–1930s some fine AAA races were held at Oakland, but when Ascot closed in early 1936 the speedway was abandoned to the West Coast outlaws. For a couple of years the races at Oakland were thoroughly forgettable, but in 1938 Charlie Curryer took over as the manager, and under the sanction of the American Racing Association (ARA) things got lots better. Curryer promoted successful hundred-mile and 200-mile races and then announced that he'd run a 500-miler starting 33 cars.

It is doubtful that there were 33 big cars on the entire Pacific Coast. How many could be expected to run 500 miles? The wily Curryer had an ace up his sleeve. He painted a white line on the race track and decreed that cars must stay above it during competition. Thus, he had a mile and one eighth oval (white line or not, it wasn't close to that figure). Actually the racing groove was above the white line anyhow, but by Curryer's arithmetic "only" 444 laps would be required to complete the 500 miles.

A suspension bridge was built for infield access during the six-hour-long 500-mile races. Publicity releases stated that the bridge was "Designed by University of California Engineering students." Actually, Oakland Speedway maintenance man Pop Evans just plain built the bridge—it worked just fine! (Welch collection).

Top left: Hal Cole in #18 goes around Bud Sennett in the #B-2 car owned by J. C. Agajanian. It is a risky pass as Cole has two wheels in the loose dirt at the top of the track. *Top right:* Tex Saunders motors around Oakland in a big Studebaker two-man car that competed at Indianapolis in the early 1930s. That bashed-in tail came from a trip over the crash wall early in the race. Bill Johnson was killed in this car while practicing for this 1940 race (Top photographs—Chini collection). *Bottom:* Tex Peterson gets the winner's trophy in 1939 from promoter Charlie Curryer. Car owner Gil Pearson smiles in the middle, as well he should—his car has just won its second Oakland 500. Peterson required relief help from Rajo Jack, but he's nowhere to be seen in this photograph (Ray Hiatt collection).

On September 25, 1938, the first 500-mile race west of the Mississippi was held at Oakland before a crowd of 12,000 racing fans. Curryer managed to scrape up 28 starters: somewhat to his surprise, 10 were still running at the end of the long grind. (Ten cars finished in the 1938 Indy race) Bud Rose won the race and $1,500 for car owner Gil Pearson. Rose averaged 92.3 MPH but this was based on the erroneous one-and-one-eighth-mile track length.

The 500-mile races were also held in 1939, 1940 and 1941. Curryer, having more confidence in the endurance of the ARA's cars, changed Oakland back into a one-mile track. The 500s continued to attract good crowds to reasonably competitive races, and each year Oakland had more finishers than Indianapolis. (Admittedly, some were a hundred or so miles off the pace.) In 1939 Gil Pearson's

Rea Bray hurtles to his death during the 1941 500-mile race at Oakland. Bray's car was powered by a huge Hispano-Suiza automobile engine—he had been experiencing handling problems for many laps (Moquin collection; photograph by Chalmers Davies).

Offy (maybe a Miller?) won again as Tex Peterson required relief help from Rajo Jack late in the race. In 1940 Pearson made it three in a row with Hal Cole in the driver's seat. In 1941 Ed Barnett in a partly crippled four-port Riley was the upset winner.

The Oakland 500s were endurance races for drivers and fans alike. It required well over six hours to run the full 500-mile distance. The published winning averages were calculated by somebody very poor at arithmetic who came up with numbers of from 83 to 88 MPH instead of the true 75 to 80 MPH speeds.

With good crowds on hand each year the 500-mile races no doubt made money for Oakland Speedway. The payoffs were good for the times with a total purse, including lap prizes, of $5,300. Most of this money was up front, with the winner receiving $1,500, second $800 and third $450. By the time the tenth-place finisher got the to the payoff window it was $65, and everybody beyond 16th place got all of $25.

A few years ago I talked to Chick Lastiri, who ran in most of the 500s and, due to various problems, finished well back in the field. I asked about running 500 miles for 25 bucks. Chick replied, "We were happy." I think things have changed in today's 500-milers.

Rajo Jack

Rajo Jack's career spanned most of the years covered in *When the Earth Moved* He started racing in 1920 and was still very active in 1941. Rajo Jack was also one of the very few black race drivers.

Much of Rajo Jack's life and racing career is clouded in mystery. Not only are ten years missing, but even his true name and date of birth are uncertain. He might have been born in 1905, or some ten years earlier. His true name might have been Dewey Gatson, Roger Jack DeSota, or neither. The "Rajo Jack" came from manufacturing and selling name plates to Model T owners who ran Rajo speed equipment — or perhaps he sold Rajo parts. He was probably born in Texas but first showed up racing in the Portland, Oregon, area. A photo with mostly unreadable notes in Rajo Jack's handwriting is dated 1920. Other photos indicate that he resided and raced in Oregon in 1923 and competed at the Culver City, California, dirt track in 1924.

Rajo Jack next appears as an obviously experienced and winning driver at Silvergate Speedway in 1934. Extensive research has failed to find any evidence of where he was or where he raced in the missing ten years.

From 1934 until World War II Rajo Jack was one of the top drivers on the Pacific

Rajo Jack in 1920. The track location is unknown but it is probably in the Portland, Oregon, area. If we believe Rajo's "official" birth date he was 15 when this photograph was taken (Herman Giles collection).

Top: Rajo Jack takes a practice ride in the beautiful Famighetti Brothers car. This is South Gate (aka Southern Ascot) Speedway in Los Angeles in about 1938 (LaRosa collection). *Bottom:* Oakland Speedway in about 1939 and Rajo Jack is on the pole. This was probably a 200-mile event held on the steeply banked one-mile oval (Erwin Eszlinger collection).

Top: Rajo Jack and his wife Ruth (or perhaps Estelle) are pictured at Victoria, British Columbia, in 1938. Jack made the 1,000-mile tow from his home in Los Angeles to race at Langford Speedway. Records indicate the rear end went out and he did not get to race despite extensive pre-race publicity (Bob McMurtry collection). *Bottom:* Rajo Jack leads Mike Reilly at Calistoga, California, in 1949. Jack is driving his own Miller. This car was listed as a 220 Miller but actually was a 183 Marine Miller. (Don Radbruch collection; photograph by Russ Reed)

Coast. Most of his racing was in California, but he made trips to Portland, to Victoria, British Columbia, and at least one trip to the Midwest to race with the IMCA. He won stock car races at San Diego and on the high banks of Oakland Speedway. He and Tex Peterson combined to win a 500-mile big car race at Oakland in 1939. He won uncounted features at tracks like Silvergate and San Jose, and on the dusty horse tracks of Central California. After World War II Jack was competitive but well past his prime. If we take his probable birth date as around 1895, he was well over 50 and still keeping up with the youngsters. Rajo Jack quit racing in about 1951 and died of a possible heart attack in 1956.

His race obviously hurt him in his racing career—black drivers were discouraged, if not forbidden, to run with the AAA. Jack might have been good enough for Indy but that door was closed to him. Or was it? Rajo Jack was quoted as saying the reason he didn't try for Indianapolis was that his right eye was missing and he'd not be able to pass the physical. Jack was popular with fans and his fellow

Rajo Jack at Des Moines, Iowa, in 1951. This IMCA event was probably one of his last races. His car, which was called "Sally", looks as tired as he does. The car has now been completely restored by Bill LaRosa of Whittier, California (Marty Brightman collection; photograph by Larry Sullivan).

drivers who accepted him as a fine human being and a fine race driver. Certainly Rajo Jack was subject to racial prejudice, but, on the West Coast, things were slightly liberal. This was not so in the conservative Midwest. When Jack ran with the IMCA in 1940 he was billed as "Rajah Ramascus, the great Portuguese dirt track champion." Perhaps some prejudice still exists—for some reason, Rajo Jack is not in the National Sprint Car Hall of Fame where he belongs.

I had the pleasure of knowing and racing against Rajo Jack in 1950. He'd been one of my childhood heroes when I saw him race at Oakland Speedway. I now kick myself for not taking the trouble to know Rajo better. I do remember that one of my proudest moments as a rookie sprint car driver came when I went around Rajo Jack on the outside in a race at Salinas, California. Rajo was nearing the end of his career, and I was young and stupid.

Thanks to Marty Brightman in Iowa and Herman Giles and Warren Jones in California for help with this brief history of Rajo Jack.

Rex Mays

If you refer to Rex Mays as one of the greatest drivers in the history of American auto racing you will get little argument. You will get no argument from me—Rex Mays was, and is, my hero.

I was lucky enough to see Rex Mays race at Oakland Speedway in the mid-

1930s. I can remember that he won a hundred-mile race and then was the victor in a 50-mile race that marked the final appearance of the AAA at Oakland. Mays was back at Oakland in 1937 to put on a spectacular display of driving skill in a midget race on the banked one-mile oval.

Rex Mays began racing in his own Model T track roadster at Chowchilla, California, in 1931. A great career started rather inauspiciously as Mays went out of the consolation race with a flat tire—Ted Horn won the race. Mays was spectacular in the roadsters but often had mechanical problems. It is probable that he won only two races, with the big payoff being all of $8.00.

In September of 1932 Mays moved on to the race cars at Legion Ascot. He quickly attracted the attention of owner Paul Fromm and was soon driving Fromm's 358-cubic-inch Hispano-Suiza aircraft-engine-powered car. For the next three years Mays was one of the dominant drivers at Ascot. Most of his victories came in Paul Fromm's Winfield Rocker Arm. This Model B Ford conversion regularly beat the Millers as Mays won the AAA Pacific Southwest Championship in 1934 and 1935.

Legion Ascot closed in January of 1936 and in the subsequent years Rex Mays made a comfortable living by racing at Indianapolis and campaigning in the Midwest and the eastern states. His best finish at Indy was a second in 1940, but he won a AAA Midwest title and was twice a National Champion. Mays also starred after World War II until his tragic death at Del Mar, California, on November 6, 1949.

This is Rex Mays' first really good race car ride. Paul Fromm was the owner, and #21 is powered by half of a World War I Hispano-Suiza aircraft engine. The photograph was taken at Oakland Speedway in 1933 (Bundy collection).

Rex Mays at Legion Ascot in 1934. This is the Paul Fromm Winfield Rocker Arm car that carried Mays to many victories. This is a somewhat rare photograph—usually the car is shown as #1 and in the cream and red Gilmore Oil Company colors (Gemsa collection).

Rex Mays is remembered not only as a great driver but as an exemplary human being. His behavior, both on and off the track, was faultless. He did not drink, smoke or use profanity—a far cry from some of today's sports "heroes."

The life of Rex Mays has been documented in a yet-to-be-published book, *Pole Position: A Biography of American Race Driver Rex Mays*, by Robert M. Shilling. Shilling uses a quote by Ernest Hemingway to describe his feelings towards Rex Mays:

> Rex Mays III (usually thought of as Rex Mays Jr.) is amazed that even after 40 years people will come up to him and speak of knowing his father, of seeing him race. All of them make some variation of the comment, 'Your father was the most wonderful man in the world.' Even after all these years Rex Mays remains a hero.
>
> Hemingway wrote that, 'If you live long enough everything you've ever loved will be sullied'.
>
> Hemingway never met Rex Mays.

San Jose, 1924

Thanks to Bob Rushing of Oakland, California, there is a remarkable amount of information available on a race at San Jose, California, in 1924. Rushing lent me a scrapbook-photo album that belonged to long-ago racer J. A. (Jim) Smith.

The race was sanctioned by a rather mysterious group called the Western Racing Association. In 1924 this organization raced in places like San Jose, Reno, Salt Lake City, and Medford, Oregon. It also had several races at the Tanforan horse track a few miles south of San Francisco. All of these races were AAA-sanctioned, so the reason for the Western Racing Association designation is unclear. Maybe it is because some of the races were apparently hippodromes and the AAA claimed it didn't put on fake races.

The San Jose race was on September 1, 1924, and drew an announced crowd of 16,000. Ralph DePalma and Eddie Hearne were there with their Millers as were some lesser AAA drivers. The field was supplemented by local cars and drivers—including Jim Smith. DePalma might have been a bit past his prime but he dominated on that day. He won four races and took home a reported $4,000.

Ralph DePalma at San Jose in his Miller Eight. DePalma did not race at Indianapolis in 1924. Is it possible that he was in trouble with the AAA in that year? (Bob Rushing collection).

Top: Eddie Hearne was one of the top AAA drivers who raced at San Jose in 1924. Although Hearne drove a #1 car at Indianapolis that year this does not appear to be the same car. *Bottom:* Eddie Hearne in #1 and Ralph DePalma get started at San Jose. Look at the crowd! San Jose was a banked five-eighths-mile oval (Both photographs—Bob Rushing collection).

Jim Smith? He crashed his Model T-based car. Smith's possible resentment of the high priced competition is seen in the photo of De Palma and Hearne. Scrawled across one corner, with apparent anger and sarcasm, is "$20,000 Miller Cars."

The races at San Jose were not without tragedy, as popular West Coast driver Adolph Guisti was killed in a crash.

Top: Adolph Guisti at San Jose on September 1, 1924. Guisti died in a crash on this day. *Bottom:* The field gets the green flag at San Jose. DePalma is on the inside, Hearne in the middle in #1, and that could be Eddie Wonderlick in #14. Car #3 looks like a AAA car but is apparently running a bit sick. The cars at the right appear to be local machines. (Both photographs—Bob Rushing collection).

Jim Smith's adventures at San Jose are depicted in these two photographs. In the first Smith poses proudly in what looks like a brand new Smith Special. In the second photograph the remains of #3 are shown on the transporter. Smith's payoff that day was almost certainly zero. (Both photographs—Bob Rushing collection).

Seattle

It was tough drawing big crowds during the Depression years, but a series of races in Seattle did just that in 1931 and 1932 at the Seattle Civic Stadium. The facility was the home of the Seattle Pacific Coast League baseball team. Night races during the late summer and fall attracted crowds of up to 10,000.

The track was a one-fifth-mile dirt—unusually short for the era. No doubt it would have been more suitable for midgets, but these cars did not exist in 1931–32. The races attracted good fields of cars from Washington and Oregon and even an occasional California visitor. For one event Legion Ascot drivers Nick Martino and Swede Smith were advertised to appear and race against locals like Mario Bianchi and Dutch Snider.

The Civic Stadium was centrally located in Seattle and this helped attract the crowds, but the secret to the success of the races was the admission price—one thin dime! The standard admission might have been 50 cents or so, but promoter Elwin

The field is lined up before a huge crowd at the Seattle Civic Auditorium in 1931. Swede Smith is on the pole with Dutch Snider on the outside. Smith had been racing at Legion Ascot but was originally from the Seattle area and a 1929 Pacific Northwest Champion (Chuck Harring collection).

Snyder flooded the city with ten cent coupons that were easily available from Seattle merchants. The purses for at least some of the races were $400, with $100 to win the feature.

Just how many races were held in 1931 and 1932 is not known—most likely the events had to be scheduled around baseball games. All went well until October 6, 1932, when a crash took the lives of Ray Dudley and Dutch Snider. Legend has it that the Seattle City Council, shocked by the double tragedy, promptly passed a law forbidding auto races within the city limits of Seattle. A good story but almost certainly not true. Races were held at the Civic Stadium after the Dudley-Snider crash, and other races have been held in Seattle over the years.

South Gate

Legion Ascot could never be replaced—perhaps it still hasn't been. The famed oval was superseded by another Los Angeles–area track a few months after it closed in 1936. This was Southern Ascot, aka Southern Speedway—a flat half-miler usually remembered as "South Gate" from its location in that Los Angeles suburb.

Pat Cunningham in a nice-looking modified at South Gate in 1936. It is unclear why this class of race car was quickly phased out in Southern California (Rod Eschenburg collection).

Top: Late 1936 action at South Gate as Rajo Jack leads an unidentified driver in #58 and a pair of modifieds. That railroad bridge shows up in numerous South Gate photographs. It is still there! (Herman Giles collection). *Bottom:* Bill Lipscomb drove this nice looking big car at South Gate and other California tracks. Lipscomb had a shot at Indy in 1940 and 1941 but failed to qualify an outdated two man car (Bill Lipscomb collection).

Bud Rose ducks as he slides into Bayliss Levrett at South Gate. The flat turns of the half-miler led to lots of action, but serious accidents were rare (Levrett collection).

South Gate gave southern California fans some racing, but it never hosted a major AAA event. Sanctioning bodies varied as modified roadsters, big cars, stock cars, jalopies and midgets raced on an oiled dirt surface that was later paved. The first races at South Gate were for modified roadsters—quickly called simply "modifieds." (These cars were the grand-daddies of the numerous classes of modifieds that race today.) The modifieds apparently drew fine crowds and put on good races, but they were quickly phased out in favor of the big cars. During the time South Gate operated (1936 to 1942) most of the racing was with big cars with local heroes like Bud Rose, Rajo Jack and George and Hal Robson winning a lot of races. The stock cars were also popular at South Gate and a couple of long distance events were won by, of all things, French Citroëns—their front-wheel-drive units pulled them around the flat turns faster than the American cars. Most of the South Gate midget races were early in 1942, when wartime restrictions prevented Gilmore from running at night.

An interesting interlude in South Gate's history took place in 1938 and 1939 when jalopy races were held on a rough road course partly in the infield. The jalopies were stripped 1920s stockers that varied from Fords and Chevys to Buicks and Cadillacs and even a Bugatti. The races were part competition and part comedy. The cars shed pieces as they bounced over the deliberately primitive course while the drivers hung on for dear life. Despite the low speeds the danger was evident, and the races ended when big car driver Bud Minyard was killed during a race.

Top: The three Robson brothers all raced at South Gate. Hal (left) had a long and successful career that included six Indy appearances. George (center) won the 500 in 1946 but, tragically, died at Atlanta a few months later. Jimmy (right) quit racing after a serious crash at Oakland in 1941 (George Sowle collection). *Bottom:* Don Farmer rides his '27 Chevy like a bucking bronco as it bounces through a South Gate turn in 1939. For unknown reasons it appears that none of the jalopy drivers used seatbelts—this contributed to Bud Minyard's death in one of these open cars. Don Farmer later moved on to the midgets and won a lot of races. (Tom Luce collection from Don Farmer Jr.)

The Chrome

One of the most famous cars on the Pacific Coast is known simply as "The Chrome." Some say it was the first car ever built by Frank Kurtis, but he might have built only the body. The lavish use of chrome plating made the car stand out at any race track. Leonard DeBell, proprietor of Atlas Chrome Plating in Los Angeles, was the first owner—then it was the Atlas Chrome. In 1936 the car was sold to Neeley Burkitt in Portland and became the Burkitt Chrome. Later on the car was remodeled, had other owners, and lost a bit of its personality, but mention "The Chrome" to any West Coast oldtimer and he will know what you are talking about.

It appears that the Atlas Chrome Special was built in 1935 and raced at Legion Ascot and Oakland speedways. Drivers included Ted Horn, Jimmy Wilkerson and Frank Wearne. No doubt the car was competitive, but with a Cragar DOHC motor it is unlikely that it beat the Millers and ever won a feature race. When Ascot closed early in 1936 the car was sold to Neeley Burkitt and driver Frank Wearne came along with the deal. Burkitt wanted to win the Pacific Northwest Championship and paid Wearne the princely sum of $25 per week plus a percentage of the winnings. Even though competition in Oregon and Washington was tough, with an influx of Ascot cars and drivers, Wearne earned the championship for Burkitt.

The beautiful Atlas Chrome Special was nearly new when this photograph was taken at Oakland Speedway in 1935. Jimmy Wilkerson is the driver. Later on owner Leonard DeBell chromed the frame rails and other parts (Wendell Bundy collection).

For the next several years the Burkitt Chrome was campaigned in the Pacific Northwest with a variety of drivers. The car made at least one trip to run with the IMCA in the Midwest and a couple of trips to Oakland Speedway. The midgets had just about killed the big cars in Oregon and Washington so it is probable that "The Chrome" didn't see much action.

The car next appeared in northern California after World War II under the ownership of Art Shanoyian. At some point it was extensively remodeled and sported a new nose and a tail with a headrest. I raced against this car around 1950 and only recently did I realize it was the Atlas-Burkitt Chrome.

The car still exists in Stockton, California. "The Chrome" deserves to be restored to its former glory.

Opposite top: Frank Wearne has put the Burkitt Chrome on the pole for this race at Aurora Speedbowl near Seattle in 1936. Wearne won features in both Oregon and Washington on his way to the championship in that year (Eckert collection from Pike Green). *Bottom:* "The Chrome" was badly wrecked at Oakland during the running of the 1939 500-mile race. Chick Barbo was running well among the leaders when a right front tire failure sent him over the wall, through a couple of fences, and nearly out onto an adjacent highway. Barbo miraculously escaped with minor hurts (Wendell Bundy collection).

2

Mountain States
Montana, Idaho, Wyoming, Nevada, Utah, Colorado

There was not much pre–World War II racing in this vast area of the United States. What little there was has, for the most part, been long forgotten. Considerable effort was put into research in this area but the results were more than disappointing.

Racing took place in the big population centers like Denver, Boise, Reno, Salt Lake City, and half a dozen Montana cities. Boise had intermittent racing from 1915 to 1940. Reno had a AAA race promoted by the Western Racing Association in 1924, and there might have been some sort of race in 1926.

In Utah there was racing at the Salt Lake City State Fairgrounds in 1915, and the AAA-WRA was there in 1924. In 1921 there was a strange match race between the very well-known Ira Vail and Clair Sprague at an amusement park called Lagoon near Salt Lake City. Sprague was billed as the "Intermountain Auto Racing Champion"—if this was for real, and not a publicist's hype, there is an awful lot of Rocky Mountain racing history missing. As for Ira Vail, he must have been on some sort of barnstorming tour of the West, but no other match races have turned up.

Wyoming had some road racing at Sheridan in 1915 and plans were announced to build a two-mile oval for auto and motorcycle racing. Odds are this never happened.

In Montana there a race at Missoula in 1916, and early 1920s racing at Billings, Helena, Great Falls, Livingston and Missoula. Quite possibly the IMCA raced in these cities annually as the Great Northern Railroad gave access to the nearly roadless area. Later on there was racing in the eastern Montana towns of Miles City and Sidney. This was in 1937 and is documented in newspaper clippings. The racers were from North and South Dakota. Sanction for the races in unclear but it was probably not IMCA. Odds are that these racers made other Montana trips that have been forgotten.

Top: The field takes the starting flag at Denver's Overland Park in about 1920. Although built for horse racing this one-mile oval hosted some fine auto races for many years (Leroy Byers collection). *Bottom:* An airplane races two cars at Helena, Montana in about 1920. This is almost certainly an IMCA event and that is probably Ben Gotoff on the outside in #8 (Tom Saal collection).

Top: Ray Gardner at Dupont, Colorado, in 1923. This is probably a different location from the later (1932–1941) Dupont Speedway. Dupont is about ten miles northeast of Denver and has pretty much been swallowed up by that city. *Middle:* Fred Merzney leans over the radiator of his Fronty bobtail at Dupont in 1923. Merzney was a top driver in the Denver area throughout the 1920s. In 1932, he had a shot at Indy in the Coleman four-wheel-drive Miller but failed to qualify (Top and middle photographs—Gardner collection). *Bottom:* A good crowd is on hand at Overland Park for this race in about 1925. It is probably a race for local cars, although a couple of the machines look like Pikes Peak or maybe even Indy cars (Leroy Byers collection).

2. Mountain States (MT, ID, WY, NV, UT, CO)

In Colorado there was more racing and there is more information. There was racing at Denver's Overland Park from 1907 until 1931. This was a one-mile horse racing track. Barney Oldfield set a track record in 1907 of 52.2 seconds. This record was broken in 1923 by the IMCA's Sig Haugdahl in his huge Wisconsin Special.

In 1925 Overland Park hosted a AAA race for an advertised purse of $10,000. Drivers like Ralph DePalma, Leon Duray, Harry Hartz, Earl Devore and Red Shafer competed in Miller and Duesenberg Indy cars. Most of the drivers had raced the same cars the previous weekend at Laurel, Maryland—a cross-country trek worthy of NASCAR today. Seven cars lined up for the hundred-mile feature event. Mechanical ailments, amid blinding dust, took their toll and only two cars finished. De Palma won by a narrow margin over Devore—perhaps a bit of hippodroming?

The AAA race was supported by local drivers who took part in "light car" events. The Drivers included Ray and Chet Gardner, 1922 Pikes Peak winner, Noel Bullock and Fred Merzney. Most of the Overland Park races over the years were for local cars and drivers.

During the 1920s the Overland Park–based locals raced at other Colorado ovals. Races are known to have taken place at Colorado Springs, Pueblo and Rocky Ford. (They might have ventured over into Wyoming, but if so, the information is long lost.)

In 1932 Dupont Speedway was built a few miles northeast of Denver. It was at first a five-eighths-mile dirt track but soon became one of the nation's first paved ovals. At some time in the mid–1930s the IMCA ran its first pavement race at

This is the impressive entrance to Overland Park—complete with filling station. The facility was built in about 1907 for the horses (Leroy Byers collection).

Dupont. The Dupont races were mainly for local drivers but racers from Nebraska and Kansas also raced there. The track operated up until World War II.

(Most of the information on Denver racing came from a scrapbook–photo album kept by racer Ray Gardner. His son, Howard—a fine 1950s driver in his own right—was kind enough to lend me the material.)

Top: Vic Felt is shown in the bobtail that earned him the AAA Rocky Mountain Championship. This is also an excellent view of the Overland Park one-mile oval. *Middle:* The date of this Vic Felt photograph is uncertain but that is probably Felt's 1929 AAA Rocky Mountain Championship trophy. Felt was a top driver in the area and later a winning car owner. *Bottom:* A pit scene at Overland Park in 1926. Note the leather strap around the front axle and spring. This was to stiffen the spring rate—things are a bit more refined these days (All photographs—Leroy Byers collection).

Top: This photograph was taken at Victoria, B.C., in 1938, but the car is identified as "the former Earl Brunk Montana State Championship car." Brunk's name shows up in various early 1930s race publicity pieces as the Montana State Champion. Where he won this honor is unknown—or maybe it is just publicist's hype (McMurty collection). *Bottom:* Lloyd Axel's name is misspelled on this photograph but this 1933 win at Dupont Speedway might have been the first of uncounted wins for the talented Axel. He was a star in Rocky Mountain big cars and midgets for decades (Stan Lee collection).

Top: It is 1965 and Lloyd Axel is still winning races. He came out of a ten-year retirement to show the kids the way home at Greeley, Colorado. Shown with a very happy Lloyd Axel are (left to right) car owner Bud Shearson, flagman Andy Anderson, trophy queen Sharon Downing, and pit steward Mearle Holbrook. *Middle:* Dupont Speedway in about 1935. Gus Schrader is on hand with his own #5 Miller—this is one of the few times Schrader ever raced on pavement. Midwestern driver Sam Hoffman is in #24. *Bottom:* The whole gang gets together to pose for this 1935 Dupont photograph. At the left is Lloyd Axel in the Harvey Ward Miller. On the right Vic Felt is seated in his own Hisso (All photographs—Leroy Byers collection).

2. Mountain States (MT, ID, WY, NV, UT, CO)   75

Top: Clyde "Tiny" Gilbert wins a trophy at Dupont Speedway in about 1937. Gilbert won a lot of races in the 1930s—this one in the Lloyd Fisher Fronty. Is that Gus Schrader wearing the sun helmet in the background? *Middle:* Harry Hart at Merchants Park in Denver in 1937. This is a cut-down big car and the 176-cubic-inch Fronty T engine is in place. Hart reportedly beat some Offys with this car. *Bottom:* Walt Killinger in his own car at Dupont. Killinger usually left the driving to others but fielded cars that raced all over the country—from Pikes Peak to Langhorne (All photographs—Leroy Byers collection).

Top: Like many others, Duke Dinsmore paused to race in the Denver area on his way east in 1937. Dinsmore pretty much stayed in the Midwest during the remainder of his career. He had Indy appearances from 1946 to 1960 (Stan Lee collection). *Middle:* Bob Verbeck owned this nice-looking car but the driver is unknown. The photograph was taken in 1937 outside Merchants Park—the Denver midget track. *Bottom:* Vic Felt is shown in his Hisso in 1934—this car was raced up until at least 1941. The Norberg Machine Shop was active in Colorado racing for many years and, at one point, manufactured a DOHC midget engine similar to the Offy (Middle and bottom photographs—Leroy Byers collection).

2. Mountain States (MT, ID, WY, NV, UT, CO)

The Alan Track

It is probable that 90 percent of the 1920s and 1930s racing took place on tracks designed for horse races. Most of this was on half-mile county fair ovals, but some auto racing was on tracks comparable to the major horse tracks in operation today. A law passed in 1910 made a number of tracks available for auto racing in various parts of the country. This was a federal law prohibiting horse racing and it was

This advertisement appeared in the Spokane, Washington Spokesman Review on May 30, 1921. Pictured is the Romano Special which won the 1916 Pikes Peak Hill Climb. Mario Bianchi drove the Curtiss–aircraft–engined car to an easy win (Don Radbruch collection).

ratified by most states. (It is quite possible the law only forbade betting on the races—but horses never race when there is no betting.)

The Alan Track was built for horse racing in northern Idaho near Post Falls, this was about 30 miles from Spokane, Washington, the major population center in the area. The track opened in 1910 and, despite the federal law, held horse races for several years. Perhaps Idaho had not ratified the law? No doubt politics had a lot to do with it, but in about 1912, Idaho did outlaw betting on horse races. The owners of the Alan Track were stuck with a very expensive racing plant.

In an attempt to keep the Alan Track solvent, other sporting events were held. Boxing matches and motorcycle races attracted fair crowds but the most successful events were auto races. In 1916 the Alan Track hosted AAA sanctioned races for a purse of $2,000. Despite the relatively remote location, the race attracted a fair field of cars as Gus Duray won before a crowd of 5,000.

For unknown reasons there was not another auto race at Alan until 1921. This time the sanctioning body was something called the Inland Empire Automobile Racing Association and a purse of $3,600 was posted—that was a "LOT" of 1921 dollars! The race attracted a reported 8,000 fans and the winner, Mario Bianchi, took home $1,000. This was the last auto race at the Alan Track. The grandstands burned down sometime in the late 1920s and the horses never did return to Alan.

Bonneville Speedway

While hardly a dirt track, Utah's Bonneville Speedway—the Bonneville Salt Flats—was active in the 1930s. It is more famous for the land speed record straightaway runs but it was also a circle track—a big one: ten to eleven miles around.

The vast expanse of salt in the western Utah desert was first used as a raceway in 1914. Promoter Ernie Moross was in Salt Lake City with eight or ten cars for some barnstorming auto races—possibly AAA-sanctioned. Local businessmen arranged for an exhibition run on the Salt Flats by the stars of Moross' troupe, Teddy Tetzlaff and the famous Blitzen Benz race car. Tetzlaff, the Benz and 150 spectators were hauled 125 miles westward by railroad. A one-mile course was measured off and Tetzlaff proceeded to break the existing land speed record by roar-

Teddy Tetzlaff and the Blitzen Benz on the Bonneville Salt Flats in 1914 (Photograph from *Salt of the Earth* by Ab Jenkins and Wendell Ashton).

ing across the salt at 141.73 MPH. (The record was not recognized by the AAA or any international group.)

Some two decades passed before Bonneville was once again used as a speedway. This time it was Salt Lake City resident and future mayor, Ab Jenkins, who ventured out onto the salt. Jenkins laid out a ten-mile circular course on the rock hard salt flats. Driving a stripped and modified Pierce-Arrow V12 roadster he set an unofficial 24-hour record in 1932 and then returned in 1933 to set an official mark of 117.77 MPH. Jenkins later built special cars, dubbed the "Mormon Meteors," that were powered by huge aircraft engines. By 1940 he traveled an amazing 3,868 miles in 24 hours—an average speed of 161.1 MPH. During the run he set a closed course record of 189 MPH for one eleven-mile lap—a record that stood until Indy and NASCAR racers went faster decades later.

Over the years other endurance records, mostly with stock cars, were set on the circular Bonneville Speedway, but nobody came close to Ab Jenkins' records.

Colorado Springs

In 1932 a series of five races was held in Colorado Springs at what was described as a "poorly built" track at the Rodeo Grounds. The races were dominated by Pat Cunningham in the Leonard Kerbs K-1 out of Otis, Kansas. Cunningham won all

Art Martinson raced this nice-looking Miller at Colorado Springs in 1932. Not too much is known about Art Martinson but he does appear at some 1930s IMCA events in the Midwest. The car, with Mel McKee at the wheel, took part in Legion Ascot races in 1933 (Stan Lee collection).

five feature events although he did have some competition from Art Martinson in at least one event. Martinson drove the only Miller to appear at the races; reportedly, the car had "too much soup" for the track.

The sanctioning body for the Colorado Springs races is unknown but the same group of drivers raced at Dupont Speedway and, apparently, other Colorado tracks.

Missoula, Montana

Although quite remote from the rest of the country, this western Montana city had racing on an intermittent basis from 1916 to 1924.

The first races were in 1916, and although the whole thing sounds like IMCA, it was reportedly sanctioned by the Western Auto Racing Association and/or the Panama Pacific Racing Association. A purse of $2,000 was posted and drivers like Ben Gotoff and Jerry Wonderlick were on hand. Also making an appearance was Barney Oldfield's famed front-drive Christie Special. This machine must have been quite tired by 1916, but it was driven by a Captain Kennedy in a special half-mile

Newspaper publicity for the 1916 Missoula races was excellent, although the headline writer went a bit overboard. Since this was most likely the first auto race ever held in the state it was bound to be the "Greatest Race Meet in History of Montana" (Dud Burnett collection from the *Daily Missoulian*).

time trial. Kennedy's time was 36.4 seconds—some five seconds per lap faster than the published times for the remainder of the races.

The IMCA was in Missoula in 1920 and here things get a bit mysterious. None of the drivers entered are familiar names. Instead the pre-race publicity centered on "foreign" drivers such as Ernie Foanpaugh of Antwerp, Belgium, Leon Delvenux of France, Jimmy Costa of Turin, Italy, and Larry D. Stone of Liverpool, England. Stone was for real but probably not from England—the other guys sound like IMCA hype. Maybe they were well-known drivers—but in Montana, foreign names were better press?

The Missoula fair hosted stock cars from 1921 to 1923 but the IMCA was back in 1924. Once again the entry list, with the exception of Paul Clancy, consisted of unfamiliar names plus some strange sounding French and Italian names. Babe Adams won the feature race followed by "Felix De Schanck, the heady French pilot." The 50-mile feature was spread out over two days of racing and the advertised purse was $7,500.

Sprinkled among the Missoula data was information that the IMCA, at least in 1920 and 1924, had races at other Montana cities. 1920 races were held at Billings and perhaps Livingston. In 1924 a point system for Northwest races was publicized—Babe Adams collected 250 of his total 1,075 points at Missoula.

(Thanks to Dud Burnett of Stevensville, Montana, for the microfilm research that supplied the above information.)

Noel Bullock at Pikes Peak

Oval-track cars have not competed in the Pikes Peak Hill Climb for a couple of decades. Like all forms of today's racing, the race up this 14,110-foot Colorado peak has become specialized beyond belief. The race was first held in 1916 and for the first forty or so years oval track cars and drivers competed on nearly equal terms with the relatively few specialized cars and drivers who ran only this race.

The story of Noel Bullock and the 1922 Pikes Peak race is worth telling. Noel Bullock began racing in 1918 near his home town of Ord, Nebraska. He started with a near-stock stripped Model T that he had built himself. Over the next few years he gradually made improvements to the car and won dozens of races on the dusty ovals of Nebraska and Colorado. By 1922 Bullock had the latest Rajo OHV head on his tiny 975-pound racer and he headed for Pikes Peak.

Noel Bullock faced competition that appeared to outclass his rather rough bobtailed T. Most of the cars entered in the AAA-sanctioned event had far bigger engines. There were racers like a Hudson, a Packard and a couple of potent Mercers. Harry McMillen, who owned, not only the Pikes Peak Highway, but also the luxurious Broadmoor Hotel, entered the Broadmoor Yellow Devil—a huge Pierce-Arrow. Bullock had only one test run up the mountain but that didn't stop him from setting the fastest time on race day and winning $500 and the Penrose Cup. His time of 20:51 was some fifteen seconds faster than King Rhiley who was second in a Hudson.

Noel Bullock is shown in the tiny Rajo T that won the 1922 Pikes Peak Hill Climb. Bullock reportedly chalked up 150 dirt track race victories before retiring at the age of 25. He then went into the aviation industry and subsequently formed his own airline. He died in a 1934 airplane crash (Gardner collection).

The fans loved Noel Bullock's victory! They could relate to the "flivver" beating the big, expensive cars. The promoters and the officials of the always pompous AAA felt differently. This was billed as a world class race and people like the main sponsor, millionaire Spencer Penrose of the *Denver Post*, did not like a lowly Ford outclassing the competition.

The next meeting of the Contest Board of the American Automobile Association took care of the problem. The rules for the 1923 Pikes Peak race established a minimum weight of 1,600 pounds for all classes of cars entered. The AAA issued this statement: "The establishment in 1923 of a minimum weight limit in each of the three classes of cars entered insures a better motor test and makes the hill climb more of a sporting proposition than it ever has been." Yeah, sure!

Noel Bullock went along with the rule change and prepared to defend his Pikes Peak championship in 1923. He cast a 625-pound babbitt weight that could be bolted under the seat of the racer and showed up for the Labor Day race. It was then that the AAA administered the fatal blow. Bullock was banned from competing because he had competed in an unsanctioned race at Sturgis, South Dakota, in July.

The AAA had taken care of the "flivver" problem at Pikes Peak.

The Gardner Brothers

While Chet Gardner is the best-known member of the Gardner clan, he is but one of a family that has been racing for over 75 years.

It was the first generation of Gardners, Ray, Chet and Dean, that raced in the 1920s, '30s and '40s. Ray's sons carried on in the second generation of racing Gardners. Howard and Jack starred in the California Racing Association (CRA) roadsters and sprints, with Jack winning the 1954 CRA championship. Ray Gardner's grandsons, J.D. Clark, Jack Gardner Jr., Jeff Gardner and Jimmie Gardner, are all involved in present day racing. Great-grandsons, James O. and Chet Gardner are crewing on a sprinter and itching to drive. So far as racing goes—Gardners are forever?

Ray was the first Gardner to race, beginning his career in 1922. Ray had his own hot Rajo Model T bobtail and competed in Colorado, Kansas, Nebraska, New Mexico, Texas and Arizona throughout the 1920s. A better-than-average driver, Ray won his share of races including the Bisbee cup at Douglas, Arizona, in 1927. Ray and his wife Augusta had five children, so family responsibilities soon dictated that Ray cut down on his race driving, even though he did compete at Legion Ascot in the early 1930s and made at least one barnstorming trip to the Midwest. He owned race cars and, as a fine mechanic, was in demand at Indianapolis up until the 1960s. Ray Gardner drove his last race at Oakland Speedway in 1939 where

Ray Gardner at Dupont, Colorado, in 1923.

Top: Chet Gardner at Overland Park, Denver, in about 1926. Gardner had been running the car as a bobtail, but this was a AAA race and tails must have been required. Despite competition from the AAA's best cars and drivers the Gardner brothers did OK at Overland. *Bottom:* The Ray and Chet Gardner racing team on the way to Texas in 1927. These transporters are near state-of-the-art, but one can only imagine the difficulty of traveling in those days (Both photographs—Gardner collection).

he won a hundred-mile race—a race wife Augusta did not know about until it was over.

Chet Gardner started racing in 1924 and his first race was probably at Overland Park in Denver. Chet followed much the same racing path as Ray and the two of them raced as a team. The Gardners moved to the Los Angeles area in the late 1920s and Chet was a big part of the racing at legendary

Right: Ray Gardner is shown after winning the hundred-mile feature event at Oakland Speedway in 1939. Gardner won over a very good field of American Racing Association cars and drivers (Ezslinger collection; photograph by Don Radbruch). *Below:* Chet Gardner is shown in his Miller in 1937. It is believed this car eventually passed into the hands of Bill Sheffler who raced it at Indy in 1946 and was later killed in the car (Gardner collection).

Legion Ascot until that track closed in 1936. Gardner was at Indy for the 500 from 1929 to 1938 with his best finish a fourth in 1933. Chet Gardner was the 1933 Midwest AAA champion and was crowned "Dixie Champion" on two occasions. He lost his life on September 3, 1938, at Flemington, New Jersey, when he crashed avoiding a child who ran on to the track.

The third racing Gardner brother, Dean, did not race as much as his older brothers. He had his own Offy midget in 1940 and raced at South Gate and other Southern California tracks. He was killed in what has been described as a "junky Ford midget" at Phoenix on October 3, 1946.

(Thanks to Howard Gardner of Bakersfield, California, for most of the information on the Gardner family.)

The WOIRA

This sounds like a town in New Zealand, but actually it stands for the Washington Oregon Idaho Racing Association. This group existed in the early 1920s and did race in all three states with some events co-sanctioned by the AAA.

WOIRA promoter Red Gardner apparently drove in his own races. He's shown here probably in 1923 and probably in downtown Boise. The make of the race car is unknown but it is not the normal Model T Ford–based car of the era.

Data are available for 1923 races in Boise and for one race in Baker—about 120 miles north of Boise. The races were promoted by a Red Gardner with fields of less than 10 cars. All the drivers were from southern Idaho and none are familiar names.

Gardner did a good job with pre-race publicity for races at Boise on July 4 and 5, 1923. Newspaper accounts a month before the races reported that the "track was being watered and graded twice a week to assure a perfect racing surface." A fair-sized crowd was on hand for the July 4 races, but it turned out that Gardner's "perfect racing surface" was pure promoter hype. The dust was so thick racing speeds were impossible. Only 200 people showed up the next day and most of the races were cancelled.

3

Southwest

Arizona, New Mexico, Texas

This is a big chunk of the United States, but with the exception of Texas there wasn't much between-the-wars racing.

In Arizona most of the racing took place at the State Fairgrounds in Phoenix. Here, racing started in 1910 on the one-mile oval that operated until 1963. At the same site there were half-mile and five-eighths-mile ovals that ran during the 1930s. Most of the Phoenix racing was under the sanction of the AAA with at least one visit from the IMCA and some outlaw events In the remainder of the state of Ari-

The Ray Gardner Rajo at Childress, Texas, in 1926 or 1927. The youngster is Ray's son, Buster (Gardner collection).

These were the newspaper headlines after the September 29, 1929, races at Abilene, Texas. Chet Gardner drove his #47 to victory, but made a trip to the hospital to get fragments of broken goggles removed from his eye—photograph at right. Bobby Bryan apparently survived his crash injuries (Gardner collection).

zona there were only a few race tracks. Douglas, Tucson, Flagstaff and Casa Grande ran infrequent races in the '20s and '30s. There was a race track at St. Johns in the eastern part of the state—probably in the 1920s. A one-mile oval at Scottsdale existed but the years of operation are unknown. Prescott had racing from 1935 until 1942 but this might have been the midgets.

New Mexico had even less known racing—this on two tracks in Albuquerque. A track called All-American Speedway existed from 1926 to 1946 but might have had only a handful of races. Races on August 29, 1926, and January 1, 1927, can be documented—there must have been other races. The other Albuquerque track was Hells Half Acre Speedway that was active in 1939 for at least one race. From the name of the track it might have run jalopies, so maybe New Mexico had only one 1920s and '30s race car speedway?

In Texas the first race was apparently at Mineral Wells just west of Dallas–Fort Worth in 1909. Galveston had beach racing in 1912, and several other tracks operated before World War I. The Dallas racing started at the Texas State Expo in 1924

Top: This is probably someplace in Texas in about 1935. Joie Chitwood is the driver and the car appears to be somewhat of a cross between a midget and a big car. From the background this is obviously a big car race. *Middle:* Tex West had the look of a race driver, and he was a good one. His real name was Austin E. Wetzler and he started racing in the early 1920s, switched to mostly midget racing in the mid–1930s, and starred in these cars until 1949. *Bottom right:* Joe Termin is shown in about 1932 at an unknown Texas speedway. Termin was killed at Haskell, Texas, in 1938 (Top, middle and bottom right photographs—Bob Noe collection). *Bottom left:* Pop Evans took his Flathead Model A to Flagstaff, Arizona, for a July 4, 1934, race. With Curley Mills at the wheel the Evans machine won the main event and $150 (Johnny Klann collection).

Top left: Flagstaff on July 4, 1934. Pop Evans is at the right standing by his #11 Flathead A. Wearing a kidney belt, with his back to the camera, is Earl Mansell, who won a lot of West Coast races. *Top right:* Chet Mortemore was one of the drivers in the 1934 Flagstaff race. Mortemore would become midget racing's first fatality when he was killed at Gilmore Stadium on October 25, 1934 (Above photographs—Johnny Klann collection). *Below left:* Red Hodges probably started his career in the Texas big cars in the mid-1930s. A bit later he starred in Tulsa midget racing where he won five of the first seven features in 1939. *Below right:* Pappy Noe campaigned this nice looking big car out of Albuquerque in the late 1930s. It is not known where he raced. The car was purchased by Noe in southern California (Below photographs—Bob Noe collection).

on a one-mile oval and this continued until about 1929. There was a short-lived half-miler at the same site but it was torn down in 1938 to build the Cotton Bowl. There were three other tracks in Dallas: Industrial, Love Field and Walnut Hill. Nearby Fort Worth saw racing at Arlington in about 1929. Further south, Houston had racing at the Bellaire Track, a one-and-one-half-mile oval, from 1926 until 1929. A half-mile track operated at the same site from 1924 to 1935—this was near the present location of the Astrodome. Other Houston speedways were Epson Downs, Gulf Coast and South Main—this may be the same location as Arrowhead Park Speedway, where some guy by the name of A. J. Foyt won his first race. Other Texas big cities that had early racing include Austin, Arlington, San Antonio, Waco and the rather remote El Paso where racing began in 1915. In the smaller Texas towns there was racing at a few dozen locations—places like Harlingen, Beaumont, Breckenridge, Abilene, Childress and Groesbeck.

AAA Racing in Texas

Beginning in 1921 the AAA held races in West Texas. One annual stop on this tour was Abilene. Other Texas towns that saw AAA action were Childress Wichita Falls and Breckenridge. Duncan, Oklahoma, had races at least in 1929.

To classify these races as true AAA events would be a bit of an exaggeration. It appears that the AAA sent one or two top-notch cars and drivers to the races with the balance of the field filled by the "outlaws" that the AAA so much despised. Data on just who the AAA hotshots were is not complete but in 1923 it was Red Shafer, in 1925(?) Peter DePaolo, in 1927 Fred Frame and in 1929 Chet Gardner. These drivers appeared in Millers and Duesenbergs, some of which were fresh from the Indianapolis Speedway. Even though these cars were not at their best on a short dirt track they easily outclassed the competition. The AAA drivers could simply toy with the Fronty T's and other stock-block machines.

The field gets ready for the start at Breckenridge in 1927. On the inside of the second row is Fred Frame in the same car he drove to an 11th-place finish at Indy that year. Car #7, in the center of the second row, is Ray Gardner (Gardner collection).

Top: Things get crowded in the first turn at Breckinridge in 1927. Fred Frame, in the Miller Eight, coasts along on the pole at the rear, wisely awaiting an opening. *Below:* More scenes of the 1927 starting field at Breckenridge (All photographs—Gardner collection).

Odds are that some of the AAA drivers were paid appearance money, but even if not, purses of $2,000 to $5,000 paid off handsomely to the winners. In 1927 Fred Frame won an estimated $1,500 at Abilene—probably the equivalent of fifth at Indy that year. Chet Gardner won $725 at this track in 1929. Payoffs at other Texas tracks were similar.

For the outlaws who provided the competition things weren't quite as good. Upon appearing for the first race of the series at Duncan, Oklahoma, in 1929 the non-AAA regulars were informed that they had to pay a fine of $25 for running at unsanctioned tracks. (Pat Cunningham circumvented this nicely by giving the AAA officials a check on a Missouri bank that had been closed for two years.)

Avoiding AAA fires was a popular sport among outlaw drivers. For these drivers the payoffs for the runner-up positions were not too bad—$50 to $250 at most tracks. In general the fields were short, so not too many drivers went home empty handed.

It is probable that 1929 was the last year of the AAA Texas series. The Depression, starting in 1930, hit West Texas very hard and it is unlikely that people had money for things like auto races.

(Thanks to Howard Gardner of Bakersfield, California for most of the information here. Howard's dad, Ray, and uncle, Chet, participated in some of the Texas races.)

Albuquerque, 1927

A series of races took place at Albuquerque on January 1 and 2, 1927. A dozen or so cars took part in the races on a one-mile oval that was probably All-American Speedway.

The headliners were Miller driver George Soulders, who would win Indy that year, Fred Frame in a Duesenberg and Harry Milburn in another Miller. Soulders and Frame are well known names but Milburn is a bit of a mystery. He apparently had his own Miller but confined his activities to the southwestern United States. The remainder of the entries were western

It is believed that this photograph was taken at Albuquerque on January 1, 1927. The driver of this bobtail might have been Matt Pulver (Gardner collection).

Albuquerque in 1927. This is the Chet Gardner Rajo which did quite well in the New Year's races. In the background is Chet's brother Ray's Rajo (Gardner collection).

drivers in Rajo Model Ts and the like. One local driver, Slim Harper, is listed in newspaper reports.

No data is available on the second day's racing, but on January 1, 1927, the races attracted 1200 spectators that "hardly approximated the grandstand crush of last year." The races were almost certainly hippodromes, although Rajo driver Chet Gardner did give a good account of himself in a couple of the races. Fred Frame had trouble in an early event and in the 25-mile final it was George Soulders the winner, followed by Gardner and Milburn.

Most of the drivers in the Albuquerque races had competed at Phoenix, 300 miles to the west, over the Christmas holiday. This was obviously a mid-winter tour by a few Miller and Duesenberg drivers plus the supporting cast. No sanctioning body is mentioned in newspaper reports at either Phoenix or Albuquerque, but both events were AAA sanctioned.

The Bisbee Trophy

In 1926 the Bisbee Trophy was offered to race winners at Douglas, Arizona. The whole thing was pretty much a Gardner monopoly as Chet Gardner was the first winner on the one-mile Douglas oval. On

The Bisbee Trophy today (Mary Tibbetts photograph).

1926—Ray Gardner with the Bisbee Trophy (Gardner collection).

October 2, 1926, it was Ray Gardner who took permanent possession of the impressive bronze cup by winning the 25-mile main event.

The two-foot-high, 30-pound Bisbee Trophy is still in the Gardner family and is owned by Chet and Ray Gardner's sister, Mary Tibbetts of Spanaway, Washington.

Like so many things in racing history there is a bit of a mystery behind the trophy. Bisbee is a town about 20 miles west of Douglas—a mining town that thrived in the early part of the century. Why would Bisbee provide such an extraordinary trophy for races in Douglas—a rival town? Research in both Bisbee and Douglas came up empty. Today, nobody knows why the Bisbee Trophy was awarded in Douglas.

The First Stock Car Invasion

How the stock cars hurt open wheel racing around 1950 is well known, but this wasn't the first time it happened. Information is a bit sparse, but it appears that Texas racing suffered from an invasion of the stock cars in the early 1930s. This time they were modified stock cars—the forerunners of track roadsters or "hot rods."

The Texas stock car races were open only to roadsters, and the engine rules were a bit loose. Lee Wick, who ran in these races, remembers, "They never lifted the hood. We could do anything we wanted." The modified roadsters ran at Houston,

Lee Wick drove this innocent-looking 1931 Model A Ford roadster in Texas modified stock car races. Under the hood is a very potent Cragar overhead valve racing engine—Wick won a lot of races (Lee Wick collection).

San Antonio, Dallas, Corpus Christi, Austin and El Paso—cities that were usually race car venues. Unlike modern times, the modified stock car intrusion into Texas seems to have lasted only a few years—there is no record of prewar roadster racing after the mid-1930s. Quite possibly, one reason for the decline was the emergence of the midgets.

4

Northern Plains
Minnesota, North Dakota, South Dakota

There was racing in all three of these states before World War I, with the earliest known events taking place at St. Paul, Minnesota, in 1904. Of interest is the racing on a two-mile dirt oval at Sioux Falls, South Dakota. This track ran 300-mile AAA championship races in 1914 and 1915.

In Minnesota the big event in the 1920s and '30s was the annual State Fair races in St. Paul. During most of these years (1919 to 1939) the track was a one-mile oval built for horse racing. In 1940 a half-mile oval was constructed and this track was used for many years, although it was paved (and ruined?) in 1964. Geography dictates that most of the racing in Minnesota was in the southern half of the state. Hibbing is probably as far north as any of the racers traveled. The IMCA sanctioned most of the major races in the state, with unknown groups sanctioning races at dozens of smaller towns. Some of the towns that had racing before World War II include Austin, Bemidji, Fairmont, Luverne, Mankato, Montevideo, New Ulm, and Saint Cloud.

The known racing in North Dakota is confined to relatively few tracks. Fargo had racing continuously from 1908 until 1941. Most of the racing was almost certainly under IMCA promotion. There was also racing at Bismarck, Grand Forks and at Nodak Speedway in Minot. Williston, in the far northwest corner of the state, had racing in 1914 and 1915—odds are there was racing there in later years.

Western South Dakota is rather sparsely populated, so there wasn't much racing there—Sturgis had racing at least in 1923 and 1925. In the eastern half of the state there was lots of 1920s and '30s activity. The IMCA made yearly visits to the State Fair Speedway in Huron and the Sioux Empire Fairgrounds in Sioux Falls. There were two tracks at the same site in Sioux Falls. A three-quarter-mile oval operated from 1929 to 1936 (possibly later), and a half-miler, also known as Fred Buckmiller Race Track, ran from 1939 to 1941 and then again after World War II.

Among South Dakota towns that had racing in the 1920s were Aberdeen, Eureka, Kimball, Letcher, Madison, Milbank, Plankington, Renner, Wagner

Top: This is about 1920 and probably someplace in South Dakota (Wood collection). *Bottom:* Howard McWhorter with a later car. This one has the four-banger Dodge with a Morton and Brett head (Jim Johannson collection).

and Webster. Sanctioning for these events is a total mystery—even for the IMCA some of these locations were a bit far flung. In the 1930s a group called the Northwest Dirt Track Drivers Association ran on a regular basis at Sioux Falls. They also journeyed to smaller South Dakota towns such as Milbank. Jimmy Wood was one of the top drivers in this group and a scrapbook he kept provides a bit of information and some good photos. Wood also ran IMCA with a deal from J. Alex Sloan.

Of interest in South Dakota history is the Ruskin Track. This shows up in various literature, but little real information is available and a suitable photo could

Top: Sioux Falls Speedway in 1929. Bill Permenter is on the outside, Frank Sands in the middle and Emory Collins on the pole. This is early in Collins' career, but he was already winning IMCA races. *Left:* George Kraft of Minneapolis drove this machine in 1932. Engine type is unknown (Both photographs—Wood collection).

not be found. The Ruskin Track, a one-mile oval that ran from 1914 to 1931, was located in the tiny town of Forestburg some 30 miles south of Huron.

(Thanks to Bill Wood of Fort Scott, Kansas, for allowing the photograph collection of his dad, Jimmy Wood, to be copied and used in this chapter).

Top: Milbank, South Dakota, in 1931; the racers line up at the pit gate. The transporter in the foreground is hauling a spare car. Is that Steve Kinser with his foot on the running board? *Bottom:* Doc Alridge drove this rather unsanitary machine at Sioux Falls, South Dakota in 1932. Odds are the car was originally a bobtail (Both photographs—Wood collection).

5 Robert Seitzer Minneapolis, Min.

Top: There were special races for ladies in the 1930s. This is Helen Wood, wife of racer Jimmy Wood, at West Sioux Falls. A brave lady indeed, to drive this car. Ms. Wood was kind enough to autograph this photograph in 1996. *Middle:* Robert Seitzer drove this unusual front-wheel-drive car in 1931. It was owned by Don Voge who later promoted races in Minnesota. There is no record of how the car performed. *Bottom:* Fred Dresselhuys of Wagner, South Dakota, was one of the better drivers in the area. He died in a September 2, 1932, crash at Belleville, Kansas.

Opposite top: There is no information available on this very different car that raced in 1931. The pretty young lady posing in the car is either Pearl Wood or Lindy Pierson. *Opposite bottom:* This is Bill Beardsly's car after his first race at Sioux Falls in 1931. Beardsly survived—but did he return for a second race? (All photographs—Wood collection).

4. Northern Plains (MN, ND, SD)

Bill Beardsly — Sioux Falls

Top: Ray Hebert is pictured at an unknown track in the early 1930s. Hebert died in a race car crash but the date and place are unknown. *Middle:* This is Wild Pete Peterson in the Rudy Kruck Chevy Four. The date is 1932—probably someplace in South Dakota. *Bottom:* Possibly someplace in North Dakota? The pole driver is unknown but that is Sam Hoffman on the outside. Hoffman relieved Kelly Petillo at Indianapolis in 1933 and drove the Mannix Duesenberg in 1934, but failed to qualify for the 500 (All photographs—Wood collection).

Top: Sig Haugdahl's Duesenberg is shown at St. Paul, Minnesota, in 1929. Although Haugdahl was nearing the end of his career he was still one of J. Alex Sloan's featured IMCA drivers. *Middle:* The race cars are lined up on the inside of the straightaway at Ada, Minnesota, in the mid-1930s. This western Minnesota town had racing throughout the 1930s on the county fair half-mile track (Marty Brightman collection). *Bottom:* Dave Champeau of Grand Forks, North Dakota. Champeau had a long career with the IMCA and CSRA before dying in a 1946 crash at Lincoln, Nebraska. Champeau was married to the widow of Billy Winn. It is believed that the unfortunate lady was previously married to Joe Russo (killed at Langhorne) so she became a racing widow three times (Top and bottom photographs—Wood collection).

Top: Jimmy Wood at Sioux Falls in 1937. *Middle:* Jimmie Slattery at St. Paul in 1937. Look at that crowd! This is an IMCA race during the Minnesota State Fair. Crowds of up to 32,000 were reported for these races. *Bottom:* The cars line up at West Sioux Falls Speedway in 1937. This three-quarter-mile track operated in 1936 and 1937 (All photographs—Wood collection).

Top: Jimmy Wood drove this nice-looking car in 1937. The local high school band appears to be playing in the background—a county fair at an unknown location. *Middle:* Clair Cotter of Albert Lea, Minnesota, in a two-port Riley. Cotter starred in IMCA competition after World War II. *Bottom:* Eddie Wagner drove this nice-looking car in 1936. The Wood collection contained a number of photographs taken at this track but its location is unknown (All photographs—Wood collection).

Top: Art Challender drove this Hispano-Suiza-powered car. The IMCA and other outlaw groups had no limits on engine displacement. The 358-cubic-inch Hissos competed with 176-cubic-inch Model T's (Wood collection). *Bottom:* Travis "Spider" Webb at St. Paul, Minnesota, in 1941. This was probably an IMCA event, but Webb raced with the AAA after World War II and had six starts at Indy (Roy Eaton collection).

The Fronty

Most race cars have but one "life." They for a while, and then even if not wrecked they are soon retired, cannibalized for parts, and cease to exist. Here is the tale of a South Dakota race car that has had not one, not two, but *three* lives.

This Fronty T was built in about 1928 by Kenny "Cementhead" Larson. Just how Larson acquired the rather uncomplimentary nickname is unknown—perhaps he was a bit stubborn. Larson built a very nice car using Star frame rails and Studebaker running gear. Just who drove the Fronty in South Dakota races is not certain, but in light of future events it might have been Merritt Woods. The car's racing record is not known, but odds are it was raced and competitive until the mid–1930s. At that point the car either sat out in the harsh South Dakota climate or (if lucky) in a barn someplace.

The Fronty next surfaces as a track roadster at Huron in 1948. Except for a roadster body the car was exactly as raced two decades earlier. This time it is known that Merritt Woods was the driver. He was now 65 years old and known as "Pappy" Woods. The Fronty was up against some tough competition from the South Dakota roadsters powered by flathead Ford and Mercury V-8s, a few Buicks and assorted other engines 20 years younger than the T. While Woods was not a big winner he more than

Top: Renner, South Dakota, in 1928. The Kenny Larson Fronty in action; that is probably Merritt Woods behind the wheel (Bob Stolze collection). *Bottom:* Roadster racing action from Gettysburg, South Dakota, in 1950. Merritt "Pappy" Woods was 65 years old but managed to hold his own with the Fronty (Frank Hughes-Jim Johannson collection).

The Kenny Larson Fronty in 1978 and looking better than ever. The photograph was taken at a Davenport, Iowa, vintage race car event—the Fronty ran some hot laps (Bob Stolze collection).

held his own on half a dozen South Dakota ovals—the fans loved the throaty roar of the Fronty. Roadster racing in South Dakota was over by the early 1950s and once again the Fronty was retired.

Another 20 or so years elapsed. With the growing interest in vintage race cars, the Fronty was once again rescued. Kenny Larson helped restore "his" Fronty to better than new. This photo of the car was taken in 1978, but the car still makes an occasional appearance at vintage events.

5

Central Plains
Nebraska, Kansas, Oklahoma

All three of these states hosted auto racing prior to World War I. In Topeka there was racing starting in 1902 and Omaha had racing in 1910. The North Central Kansas Free Fair at Belleville had racing starting in 1911. Oklahoma City held a major AAA event in 1915 on a two-and-four-tenths-mile course laid out on the city streets, and there were oval track races in several cities prior to World War I.

This is Senter park in Franklin, Nebraska, and the year is probably 1922 (Roy Eaton collection).

Top: Tom Garrett at Franklin on July 4, 1923. Garrett set a track record on the one-mile oval on this day—49 seconds. It is known that Garrett was killed in a race car within a year but details are missing (Rutledge collection). *Bottom:* Noel Bullock, probably at Holdrege, Nebraska, in 1922. Bullock won scores of outlaw races before winning the Pikes Peak Hill Climb in 1922 (Harold Osmer collection).

In Nebraska the IMCA raced at Lincoln during the state fair from 1915 to 1941. In the early 1920s there was racing at towns like North Platte, Holdrege, Lexington and Beatrice—racing continued at most of these towns until 1941. Franklin had a mile track that ran races at least in 1923, 1924 and 1925. In the 1930s races were held at Deshler, Hastings, Kearny, Oshkosh and Neligh. (The tiny town of Neligh, current population 1,742, is in a remote part of northeastern Nebraska; also hosted races in 1915.) A Nebraska speedway of note was located at Ord and racing started there in 1926.

Kansas had lots of racing in the 1920s and '30s. The dean of Kansas race tracks has to be Belleville. From 1911 to 1931 this half-mile track was flat—the famed high banks were built in 1932, and at one time reached a height of 18 feet—they are a little lower today. Dodge City is more famous for movie cowboys shooting each other, but it had a two-mile oval that ran national championship motorcycle races and, in 1921, one auto race. Dodge City also had a half-miler that ran from around 1934 until World War II. At the Kansas State Fairgrounds, in Hutchinson, racing started in 1914 and is still going on today. In Wichita, the Westside Track ran races in 1916 and 1921; Meridian Speedway, a mile-and-a-half square track, ran from 1921 to 1922. This same city also had the Bo Sterns Track that operated for 1928 until 1938. Topeka had a fairgrounds half-mile oval that lasted from 1902 until 1983. Among other Kansas race tracks were Anthony, Arkansas City, Council Grove, Delphos, Dighton, Goodland, Great Bend, Lawrence, Oakley, Salina, WaKeeney and Winfield.

In Oklahoma the State

Top: Probably Omaha in about 1926 as G.O. West works on his bobtail. West was killed on September 1, 1926, at Aberdeen, South Dakota (Ken Larson collection from Jim Haag). *Bottom:* John Bagley raced this Fronty out of Omaha even though this photograph was taken in Milwaukee in about 1933. That's Bert Ficken in the driver's seat (Roy Eaton collection).

Top: Another unknown car, apparently around 1930. *Middle:* Troy Pigg was from Beatrice, Nebraska, and competed throughout Kansas and Nebraska. He was killed at an unknown track in about 1932 (Wood collection). *Bottom:* An unknown driver at an unknown track. Whoever he is, he certainly looks determined! (Top and bottom photographs—Don Radbruch collection).

Opposite top: Looks like there is good field of cars present at this unknown race track. The date is the early 1930s. Leonard Kerbs reportedly built car #700 (Jack Earle collection). *Opposite bottom:* Race drivers pose for the cameraman at Neligh, Nebraska, on September 11, 1930. Left to right they are: Jinx Phillips, Curley Freeman, Rudy Mulfinger, Bert Ficken. Fred Dusselhuys, Fay Gardner, Lew Fenno, Sam Bagley and Maynard Clark with his friend "Beans." Given the casualty rate of the era it is not surprising that three of these men, Phillips, Fenno and Dusselhuys, died racing (Bob Stolze collection).

Fairgrounds in Oklahoma City saw racing possibly as early as 1913, and this continued until after World War II. Most of this racing was probably IMCA as this group made annual visits in the fall of the year. Muskogee had racing starting in 1915 on a track that still exists today. In Tulsa things got underway in 1914 and continued until 1953. The IMCA and/or the AAA might have sanctioned the Musko-

gee and Tulsa events. In other smaller cities there was 1920s and '30s racing at Ardmore, Chickasha, Duncan, Dewey, Cushing, Hobart, Lawton and Picher. It is known that some of the racing at the smaller cities was by touring groups, but the odds are that there were also local racers.

Top: Emory Collins in his own Fronty chases Pat Cunningham in the supercharged Fronty #700. It is 1934 and most likely in Kansas (Bob Stolze collection). *Bottom:* Murray Earl drove this car in early 1930s Kansas races. Earl quit driving around 1935 but was active as a car owner until the 1950s (Jack Earle collection).

Top: Waldo Barnett broke his leg when he crashed Murray Earl's car at Hutchinson, Kansas, in about 1935. Barnett was killed at Ord, Nebraska, on August 26. 1947. *Bottom right:* A group of the better-known outlaw cars were on hand for this race—probably Hutchinson, Kansas in about 1935. At the top of the photograph is the Frankland, stagger-valve Fronty, K-1 is the Kerbs Riley, #35 is the Vic Felt Hisso—looks like it was  crashed on this day—and the next car is the Morgan Miller. *Bottom left:* Waldo Barnett poses with car owner Murray Earl's son Jack in 1935. Jack Earle (the family changed the spelling) supplied a number of the photographs for this chapter (All photographs—Jack Earle collection).

Top: Some racers pose for the cameraman at an unknown Kansas track in the late 1930s. Left to right: unknown, mechanic Ted Davis, car owner Murray Earl and driver Waldo Barnett. *Bottom:* After the races someplace in Kansas or Nebraska. The black car is the Fisher Dreyer. At the right is driver Clyde "Tiny" Gilbert and the pretty lady is his wife. Despite his size Gilbert was a fine driver (Both photographs—Jack Earle collection).

Top: The fans crowd close to the pit railing as Waldo Barnett works on the car he drove at this unknown race track. *Middle:* Tex West raced at many tracks from Texas to the Dakotas. This is most likely someplace in Kansas in the mid–1930s (Roy Eaton collection; photograph by Les Ward). *Bottom:* Like many of the photographs in the Stan Lee collection this photograph is identified and dated but the track is unknown. Lee was from Denver but followed the big cars eastward into the adjacent states (Top and bottom photographs— Stan Lee collection).

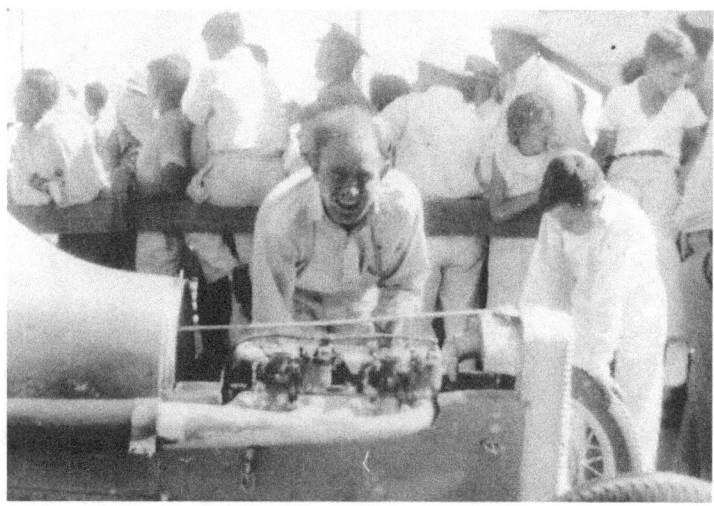

Top: Identification is far from certain on this photograph, but that looks like Lou Durant in the race car. The other man may be promoter Tom Holden (Leroy Byers collection). *Middle:* Denver driver Aaron Woodard is shown at Belleville in 1940. The track was much narrower than it is today, and from the photograph it appears to be dry and slick. *Bottom:* Cecil Burnaugh is shown with John Gerber at Belleville in 1940. Burnaugh was a fine driver and won a lot of races for John Gerber. Later on, Burnaugh bought #15 and raced it on the west coast after World War II (Lower photographs—Roy Eaton collection).

Top: Harry Hart at Anthony, Kansas, in 1937. From this and other photographs it looks like the Denver drivers journeyed eastward to race at Anthony. *Middle:* Bob Vorbeck at Anthony. Note the minimal protection for spectators. *Bottom:* Another view of the track at Anthony and this time it is Johnny Mauro. It was nice of somebody to date the photographs but it took several years of research to figure out that the photographs were taken at Anthony (All photographs—Leroy Byers collection; Stan Lee collection).

The Hatton and Hurst Circuit

One of the touring groups of racers that ventured into Oklahoma and Texas to race was the Hatton and Hurst Circuit. Thanks to Johnny Gerber in his fine autobiography, *Outlaw Sprint Car Racer*, documentation of the 1925 and 1926 tours is available. In 1925 there was racing at Frederick, Hobart and Ardmore in Oklahoma and at Childress, Texas. There is no record of any sanctioning body, but in the Hobart race was George Soulders, who was only two years away from winning the Indy 500 in 1927. Probably the most notable thing about these races was that Gerber crashed at Hobart—the only serious wreck of a long career on dirt tracks all over the middle part of the United States.

There was a similar circuit in 1926, although Hurst was out of the picture and Hatton co-promoted with Bowen and Onley. Three days of racing were scheduled for Grossbeck, Texas, for a purse of $1,000 per day. The first day only a small crowd showed up to see races on a very sandy track—the next two days were canceled. There were races at New Braunfels and Beaumont followed by three Sundays of racing at Harlingen on the southern tip of Texas. A race on the two-mile track at San Antonio finished the tour.

John Gerber doesn't mention any numbers, but it is probable that the promoters made most of the money. Gerber often won up to $500 per race but this apparently did not happen in Texas or Oklahoma.

(The amazing story of John Gerber's life is chronicled in his book. For information on *Outlaw Sprint Car Racer* contact Ed Watson at Witness Productions, Box 34, Marshall, IN 47859. (765) 597-2487.)

The Lawrence Hughes Collection

Lawrence Hughes is one of many fine race drivers who have been all but forgotten by history. Hughes raced in the 1920s and early 1930s in Nebraska, Kansas, Iowa and perhaps Oklahoma. He logged countless laps on the dusty and rutted county fair horse tracks. Hughes won more than his shares of races and was good enough to make money racing even during the depths of the Depression. The details of Hughes' exploits are long forgotten, but fortunately he left behind a large collection of photos that graphically illustrate the life of a race driver in that era.

Hughes' son, Ed Hughes of Wilsonville, Oregon, has preserved these photographs and graciously allowed them to be shared in these pages. Ed is a member of the Northwest Vintage Speedster Club and the photos are now a part of that organization's archives. Thanks are also due to club member Don Shreve for the loan of the photographs.

As with so many old collections the photos were not identified. A few drivers and a few places can be recognized, but mostly all we can do is relax and let the photos speak for themselves. Enjoy!

Top: Lawrence Hughes with one of his first cars in about 1924. *Bottom:* The mid-1920s, probably someplace in Nebraska. The driver's name is "Dick" and he has added a truss beneath the Model T frame rails (Both photographs—Ed Hughes collection).

Top: Roy Boggs campaigned on the dirt tracks of Nebraska and Kansas. Boggs was later a flagman for the Nebraska Hot Rod Racing Association. Sadly, he died when struck by an out-of-control roadster in 1950. *Middle:* Nothing is known about this car or driver. *Bottom:* Here is something different—a Buick race car. Certainly a dapper-looking driver but his name is unknown (All photographs—Ed Hughes collection).

Top: No fancy motels for these racers. Hughes and his fellow drivers simply camped out in the infield of the county fair race tracks. *Bottom:* Lawrence Hughes with a couple of friends (Both photographs—Ed Hughes collection).

Top: The Hughes race car transporter in about 1930. *Middle:* One of the few action photographs in the Hughes collection. This is almost certainly Ord, Nebraska. *Bottom:* A pit scene, possibly at Beatrice, Nebraska. The Hughie Special is Lawrence Hughes' car (All photographs—Ed Hughes collection).

The Kansas Cyclone

That's what they called Leonard Kerbs—a moniker well earned as he swept away Kansas competition in the 1920s.

Kerbs was from Otis, Kansas, where his dad operated a combination auto and farm machinery shop. With this background it was only natural that Leonard developed the skills necessary to work with machinery—and to work with race cars. Kerbs started racing in about 1915 with a flathead Model T bobtail. In later years he ran some of the better-known Model T racing equipment like Craig-Hunt, Roof-Laurel and finally Frontenac (Fronty). Kerbs used his machinist skills to convert the Craig-Hunt overhead valve unit into a double overhead cam setup in 1921. This ambitious project apparently did not work out as Kerbs was soon using the Fronty head.

Kerbs raced at Kansas towns like Albilene, Hutchinson, Great Bend and Belleville—and doubtless many others. He made frequent trips to Nebraska and Colorado and competed at Overland Park in Denver. His billing as the "Kansas State Champion" was no doubt somewhat unofficial but Kerbs was a winning driver for many years. His prowess can be gauged by the rivalry he built up with Noel

Leonard Kerbs at an unknown Colorado track in 1923 (perhaps Rocky Ford). The photograph inscription in Kerbs' wonderful handwriting reads, "Yours truly, For Faster Fronty Fords. L. E. Kerbs." (Leroy Byers collection from Les and Beryl Ward).

Top: This is Senter Park at Franklin, Nebraska, and the date is probably July 4, 1923. Franklin held auto races for several years in the early 1920s and paid purses of around $2,000. It is a safe bet that Leonard Kerbs took home his share of the cash. *Bottom:* Leonard Kerbs in his own Fronty in 1930. The #K-1 designates either "Kerbs 1" or "Kansas 1." (Both photographs—Roy Eaton collection).

Top: Pat Cunningham drove for Leonard Kerbs in 1933. Kerbs had a nice-looking truck to haul his race car, and—as is obvious—had some sponsors. Most likely the sponsorship consisted only of free parts (Roy Eaton collection). *Bottom:* The Kerbs #K-1 was sold to R.W. Caldwell in 1932 and is seen here at Neal's Speedway in San Diego. That's Caldwell in the car but Earl Mansell usually did the driving. Caldwell advertised the car for sale in 1934 for $500. It is not known who bought it, but the car just plain disappeared (Johnny Klann collection).

Bullock, the 1922 Pikes Peak winner. The two of them hooked up in a series of match races that had crowds on their feet at racetracks throughout the area. Kerbs ran dead even against Bullock. Outlaw legend Johnny Gerber usually raced further to the east, but tangled with Kerbs on a few occasions. In his autobiography, *Outlaw Sprint Car Racer*, Gerber has this to say: "At Anthony, Kansas on July 24 (1926) I won the feature. This was the first time I beat Leonard Kerbs of Otis Kansas."

Kerbs drove until 1930 when his son was born. After that he was active as a car owner with Sam Hoffman or Pat Cunningham at the wheel of his #K-1 Fronty. Later on he was race director and flagman at Belleville. Leonard Kerbs died in 1960.

(Thanks to a 1983 *Vintage Ford* article by Fred Houston of Broken Arrow, Oklahoma, for most of the information in this story).

The Musick Brothers

Does it seem that there were a lot of Musicks racing in the 1930s and '40s? They turned up in half a dozen states and in both the big cars and midgets. There were six Musick brothers and all were born in the Dallas area. No doubt a book could be written about the adventures of the Musicks, but, briefly, here's what they did in racing.

Cecil Musick. Although a racing fan and supportive of his brothers, he never raced.

Morris Musick at Dayton, Ohio, in 1936 (Don Radbruch collection).

Morris Musick. Morris started in the big cars in 1935 in the Texas based Southwest Racing Association (SRA). He soon migrated northward and raced in the CSRA and IMCA. In 1938 he drove the Iddings Hal and finished a close third in CSRA points to Jimmy Wilburn and Joie Chitwood. Morris later moved to the Denver area and was one of the top drivers in the Rocky Mountain Midget Racing Association. He retired from racing in 1950 and died in 1960 of a massive heart attack.

Ben Musick. He also started his racing career in the Texas big cars. At some point he got in trouble with the law for allegedly hijacking a liquor truck, and during the prewar years he raced under the name of Bill Morris. He placed well in the IMCA standings, but his best years came after World War II when he drove the Ralph Morgan 318 Offy to top finishes in both the IMCA and CSRA. Like brother Morris Ben quit racing in 1950. He too was claimed by a heart attack, in 1967.

Lynton (Len) Musick. Some say that Len was by far the best of the Musick bunch, and his rather brief record tends

Right: Ben Musick in an Offy owned by Gus Schrader in 1941 (Jim Haag collection—Larry Sullivan collection). *Below:* Len Musick in the Harris stagger-valve Fronty. Someplace in Illinois in 1937 (Eaton collection).

to prove this. Len began racing in 1935, and by 1937 was running fast enough to take a third place finish in IMCA point standings—this behind Gus Schrader and Emory Collins. Len had a health problem—he couldn't breathe easily. What should have been a simple operation to correct a sinus condition proved fatal; Len Musick died on the operating table at the age of 25.

Elmer Ray (Rabbit) Musick. He started his career in both the midgets and big cars in 1939. Rabbit concentrated on the midgets in the prewar years and had victories on the tough Texas circuit. Following military service in World War II he won midget races in machines like the Vito Calia Offy. In the big cars, he drove the former Gus Schrader 318 Offy then owned by Peaches Campbell. Rabbit quit racing in 1949 and moved to California, where he died in a traffic accident in 1962.

Leland Musick. Although he drove a few big cars Leland spent most of his career in the midgets. He really didn't hit his stride until after

Left: Leland Musick at the wheel of the Vito Calia Offy. This is Kansas City, Missouri, in 1948. *Below:* Rabbit Musick at Gilmore Stadium, Los Angeles, in 1947. He's in the Bill Keech Offy (Both photographs—Bill Hill collection).

World War II, when he drove Bill Himes' "Catfish" Offy to wins at several Texas and Oklahoma tracks. Crashes plagued his career, and in 1948 he was fired from his ride after three crashes in four races. Another serious crash in 1949 ended his racing career. Leland Musick died in the early 1990s.

The five racing Musick brothers carved a path of victories throughout the central United States for a decade. There was also another Musick—this was Cotton Musick, but he was from Kansas and not related to the Texas Musicks.

Ord

by V. Ray Valasek

If you've never seen an auto race between top-notchers, you've never experienced the acme of thrill. You've never lived until you've seen those graceful slender bits of mechanism propelled around a half-mile track by powerful engines and guided by men with nerves of steel. Roaring around turns four abreast, their gay colors flashing in the sun, their mighty engines roaring in unison, they approach the grandstand while thousands of spectators shout. Before you realize it they're rounding the far turn again.

If you love vigor, action, color, excitement, life itself, you won't miss these races.

—So wrote an unknown reporter for
the *Ord Quiz* on August 16, 1928

Auto racing in Ord, Nebraska, came about because of some creative thinking by E.C. Weller and Ernie Hill, members of the Valley County Fair Board. They believed that auto racing, being relatively new and exciting, offered the many thrills that would be the drawing card to make the annual county fairs a success.

The first auto races at Ord were held on September 15, 16 and 17, 1926. The *Ord Quiz* headline read, "Six Thousand Breathless Fans See Kerbs Win Sweepstakes." Leonard Kerbs won from a field that included Gus Schrader, W.H. Pingrey and John Bagley. Another headline after the 1926 races proclaimed, "Bumper Crowds Make County Fair Financial Success." Weller and Hill had been correct in their judgment of auto racing's being a good draw.

Ord racing officials were wise in their promotions of races at this relatively remote location. Clyde Baker was in charge for many years and he and his wife, Alma, traveled to other communities working out details of scheduling race meets. Programs tied in with races at Cedar Rapids, Iowa, Overland Park in Denver, Belleville, Kansas, and other smaller towns This resulted in a schedule that enabled competitors to run a number of tracks on a swing through the mid-states.

Most of the races at Ord were strictly outlaw, but the powerful AAA did sanction races in 1928 and 1930. Only 12 cars appeared for the 1928 races and the many regulations of the AAA had a detrimental effect on the program. After going out-

Above and opposite: Ord and the starting field in September of 1935. These photographs were taken early in the day—by race time the stands would be full (Leroy Byers collection).

law in 1929 Ord was once again courted by the AAA in 1930. Car count in 1930 was better than in 1928 but the autocratic rule of the AAA left the Ord racing officials believing they, with greater freedom, could promote a more exciting program and attract a greater number of cars. True! As an example, 12 cars were entered in 1928 and 38 cars appeared in 1931.

There were no races or even a fair in 1932, 1933 and 1934; economic conditions and the drought did not allow even the most optimistic individual to plan such an event. Survival during the Depression and the severe drought years was the only thing on everyone's mind.

When racing resumed in 1935 the entry list included 20 drivers and cars from 11 states. This was in the middle of the Depression—very impressive! In 1938 the addition of a one-fifth-mile semi-banked track directly in front of the grandstand allowed the running of the new and exciting midgets. These cars brought drivers never before seen at Ord. One such driver was Cal Niday. An accident involving Cal resulted in his breaking his one good leg (an accident early in his career had cost him the other leg and he used a prosthesis). My father, who was working track security, removed Cal from his car. He vividly remembers Cal telling him about his artificial leg and asking him to be careful with the broken one!

A very successful midget race was held in 1939 but 1940 and 1941 were lean years and the Valley County Fair was in such poor financial shape that no races were held. Racing resumed after the war years in 1946.

Some of the greats of racing who appeared at Ord in the 1920s and '30s were Johnny Gerber, John Bagley, Leonard Kerbs, Sam Hoffman, Archie Powell, Vic

Top: A field of the best drivers in the central United States line up at Ord on September 2, 1931. Sam Hoffman in the Kerbs DO Fronty is on the pole and is flanked by Burt Ficken in the Bagley Cragar and Pat Cunningham in the B & B blown Fronty. Row two has John Gerber in his SO Gerber, Mike Billman in the Gardner SO Fronty and Clyde Gilbert in the Fisher DO Fronty. In row three is Clarence Haskel in the Johnson DO Fronty. John Gerber won the race (Roy Eaton collection). *Bottom:* They are off and running at Ord in 1936. Action like this attracted huge crowds to the Ord track (Wood collection).

Top: This 1936 field at Ord includes Lloyd Axel, Duke Dinsmore, Clyde Gilbert, Morris Musick, Everett Saylor and Ben Musick. The banking at Ord was comparable to that at Belleville, hundred miles to the south, and the two tracks were friendly rivals (Lee collection). *Middle:* Lloyd Axel paid a visit to Ord in 1937. He's shown with owner Vic Felt in the Hisso-powered machine (Leroy Byers collection). *Bottom:* Jimmy Wood was at Ord in 1936. He was the fastest qualifier at 26.0 seconds (Wood collection)

Felt, Lloyd Axel, Gus Schrader, Emory Collins, Johnny Krieger, Andrew Fuller, Bill Spence, Bert Fisher, Clyde Gilbert, Joie Chitwood, Everett Saylor, Duke Dinsmore, Jimmy Wood, Cal Niday and Danny Oakes.

(Ray Valasek of Lincoln, Nebraska, is the leading authority on the racing at Ord. He is in the process of putting together a book on this historic track. He can be reached at 821 Driftwood Drive, Lincoln NE 68510.)

6

Midwest

Wisconsin, Iowa, Illinois, Missouri

There was an awful lot of racing in this part of the United States in the 1920s and 1930s. This was especially true of Iowa. Iowa has 100 counties; most of them had half-mile fairgrounds tracks and most of them, at one time or another, had auto racing.

In Wisconsin racing began at the Milwaukee Mile in 1903 and continues to this day. Races at Milwaukee were sanctioned by both the AAA and IMCA, and during the 1930s J. Alex Sloan was the promoter. Milwaukee also had racing on a couple of shorter ovals during the 1920s and '30s. Grant Park, on the lakefront, operated in the 1920s and the five-eighths-mile South Milwaukee Speedway ran from ca. 1928 to 1931. Other tracks that were active during the '20s and '30s were located at Cedarburg, Beaver Dam, Wausau, Oshkosh and Sun Prairie. Angell Park Speedway, at Sun Prairie, is noted as the longest-running midget track in the United States, but it did have a half-mile oval from 1938 to 1941 that no doubt hosted the big cars.

Iowa had close to a dozen tracks that ran before World War I. These included Burlington which had a AAA championship race on its half-mile oval in 1915. The Iowa State Fairgrounds Speedway in Des Moines opened in 1907 and still operates today—from 1915 to 1977 this was the home of some great IMCA races. The now-famous Knoxville Raceway ran a few races prior to World War I and was active in the 1930s. Cedar Rapids had its first race in 1925 and Gus Schrader won his first feature there in that year. In Davenport the half-miler at the Mississippi Valley Fairgrounds opened in 1920 and was a regular stop on the IMCA tour for many years. Sioux City had two different tracks at the Interstate Fairgrounds that were used for racing on an intermittent basis from 1916 to 1936. (After 1936 the site had a couple of midget speedways.) Waterloo had a one-mile oval that ran in the 1920s. An unknown number of Iowa's smaller towns also had racing. Places like Bedford (current population 1,528) held races sanctioned by unknown groups with forgotten drivers.

Top: Ernest Gayden was a chauffeur for Kansas City millionaire George Wade and also drove race cars. The racial segregation of the times (1922) dictated that Gayden probably drove in races for black drivers—just where these races were is unknown. George Wade fielded a couple of board track cars. That's George Jr. on the running board of the Revere roadster (Roy Eaton collection). *Bottom:* This is probably Aledo, Illinois, in 1925. It is not known who the lady is or who drove the car (Dick Iverson collection).

6. Midwest (WI, IA, IL, MO) 141

In Illinois the situation was much the same as in Iowa—plenty of racing and a lot of it was before World War I. At the state fairgrounds in Springfield racing started in 1910 on a one-mile oval with a grandstand facing south—not ideal for the fans' comfort. In 1929 the track and grandstand were relocated to face east and this oval is still in operation. At the DuQuoin Fairgrounds racing did not start until 1936 and this was on a half-mile track; the present one-mile track was built in 1941. In the big city of Chicago there was racing on at least 37 tracks plus a few more if suburbs in Indiana are counted. Most of these tracks raced midgets or are out of the time frame of this book. Aurora Downs, Calumet, Hawthorn, North Shore, Sparta

Right: Esthan Wenneston at the Champaign County Fairgrounds in Urbana, Illinois, on September 7, 1925. Wenneston was killed on this day. This track ran from 1925 to 1928 when the grandstands burned down—these were not replaced until 1939 (Jerry Murwaski collection). *Below:* The Interstate Fairgrounds at Sioux City, Iowa, in 1927. Sam Hoffman is in #20. This is an IMCA race and the other cars are owned by promoter J. Alex Sloan (Bob Stolze collection).

Top: Sam Hoffman drove this Kreck Cycle Shop Fronty at Sioux City. With the car is Felix Morosco, a fine mechanic even though crippled since birth (Bob Stolze collection). *Middle:* Howard "Speed" Adams in 1926. This is the ex–Gus Schrader Dodge. Adams died in a 1932 crash at Nashville, Tennessee, when he tangled with Red Campbell on a very dusty track. *Bottom:* John Bagley someplace in Iowa in 1929. Better known as a car builder and mechanic, Bagley later left the driving to others (Lower photographs—Roy Eaton collection; photographs by Larry Sullivan).

Stadium and the Cook County Fairgrounds all had racing from 1920 to 1941. Worthy of mention is the Calumet Speed Bowl that was built as a dog racing facility but never used for that. Auto races were held on a half-mile square track from the late 1920s until 1934. In the rural regions of Illinois it was the same story—racing on dozens of fairgrounds tracks.

Missouri had racing on half a dozen tracks before the First World War. This included racing at the Saint Louis World's Fair in 1903 on a one-mile circular track called the Maxwelliton Track. Kansas City had a mile and an eighth oval in 1916 and Ralph De Palma won the only race ever held there. The Missouri State Fair is held in Sedalia and racing started there on a mile track in 1915 and continues at present. Sedalia added a half-mile oval in 1936—Bobby Grim was the winner of the opening IMCA race. The other big

Top: The great Johnny Gerber in his bobtail. Gerber excelled as a designer, builder, mechanic and driver. His Whippet Special shown here is a highly modified 490 Chevy Four. *Bottom:* Three of the best line up for a race at Cedar Rapids, Iowa, in 1928. Do these guys really need any introduction? Gus Schrader went on to become a many time IMCA champion. Ernie Triplett starred at Legion Ascot and won a AAA Pacific Southwest Championship. Johnny Gerber was a legend in Midwestern racing (Both photographs—Roy Eaton collection; photographs by Larry Sullivan).

fair in Missouri is the Ozark Empire Fair at Springfield. For some reason racing did not get started there until 1937. At Saint Joseph there was racing from about 1914 to 1934—John Gerber got his start here in 1921. Some of the other larger Missouri cities that had racing include Independence, Jefferson City, Carthage, and Cape Girardeau (where Everett Saylor was killed in a dusty 1942 race.)

Top: Driver Sam Hoffman (at left) and owner Felix Morosco traveled in style with this 1930 hauler. It is believed that Morosco owned the sponsoring "Finish Store" in Sioux City, Iowa (Wood collection). *Bottom:* Gus Schrader in his own Dodge Four in 1930. It is rumored that Schrader tried to race this car with no springs. Note how low the car is—maybe there *are* no springs? The experiment failed miserably! (Harold Osmer collection).

Top: Maynard "Hungry" Clark in his own DO Fronty in 1930. Clark later had great success driving for Johnny Gerber. *Middle:* Ernie Triplett began his career in the Midwest but soon moved to Los Angeles and the big money at Legion Ascot Speedway. He ran at Indy from 1929 to 1933, with a seventh-place finish in 1931 his best effort (Emil Andres collection). *Bottom:* Emory Collins in 1931. The DO Fronty looks heavy, but under Collins' heavy foot it was no doubt competitive in IMCA races (Top and bottom photographs—Roy Eaton collection; photographs by Larry Sullivan).

Top: "Cowboy" Hardy in the Leo Krasek car at Cedar Rapids in 1930. Krasek was a better-than-average mechanic and built his own overhead-valve heads for the Ford Model B engine (Roy Eaton collection). *Middle:* Cliff Woodbury someplace in Illinois in 1930. Chet Gardner attempted to qualify this car in the 1929 Indianapolis race but had engine problems. Woodbury was a four time starter in the 500. *Bottom:* This is Emil Andre's first race car at an unknown track in 1932. As the note on the photo indicates, Andres had a rather inauspicious debut in racing. Things went a bit better later on with 12 Indy appearances (Lower photographs—Emil Andres collection).

Top: Emil Andres at Evanston, Illinois, in 1933. This appears to be the same car he wrecked in 1932 but the engine is different. This time it is a three-port Fronty. *Middle:* Fred Prentiss drove this bobtail at Sterling, Illinois, in 1934. By this date the bobtails had been pretty well phased out. The Prentiss #2 might have been one of the last bobtails to race (Harold Osmer collection). *Bottom:* The cars are pushed off for a race at Evanston in 1932. A very typical scene that was repeated hundreds of times all over the United States and Canada. (Top and bottom photographs—Emil Andres collection).

Top: Sam Hoffman smiles before a race at Cedar Rapids in 1930. One has to wonder how often that exposed carburetor was damaged by flying dirt clods. *Middle:* Gus Schrader in his own Miller in 1932. No doubt an IMCA race—possibly Cedar Rapids, Iowa (Top and middle photographs—Roy Eaton collection; photographs by Larry Sullivan). *Bottom:* Sterling, Illinois, in 1931 and Pont DeFrates in the Leeds Chevy equipped with a totally fail-safe braking system. It is too bad this advanced technology did not catch on. Can't you just see today's sprint car drivers wearing shoes with specially-developed Goodyear soles two feet wide? (Harold Osmer collection; photograph by Larry Sullivan).

Opposite top: This is Shorty Catlon at Milwaukee in 1931, driving the Schneider stagger-valve Fronty. Catlon had a long career that included Legion Ascot and 13 appearances at Indy. He died at Indianapolis in 1947 (Roy Eaton collection; photograph by Larry Sullivan). *Opposite middle:* A very dapper Gus Schrader someplace in Iowa in about 1936. With Montgomery Ward Riverside Tires as a sponsor, Schrader was able to bolt on a fresh set of those earth-moving knobbies for every race (Bob Stolze collection). *Opposite bottom:* Milt Marion was a top-notch dirt track racer in the 1930s—this photo was probably taken at Sterling, Illinois. Marion had four shots at Indy from 1931 to 1937. He usually drove his own car and failed to make the starting field (Emil Andres collection).

Top: Milwaukee in 1937 and Buddy Callaway gets ready to go in a rather ancient four cylinder Dodge. Callaway usually ran IMCA but took a shot at Indy in 1932 but failed to qualify (See the Lakes Chapter for details of this "Hisso"). *Middle:* Jimmy Snyder was one of the many great drivers who drove for Johnny Gerber. Snyder raced four times at Indianapolis and finished second in 1939. He died in an obscure midget race at Cohokia, Illinois, on June 29, 1939. At the time of his death he was the lap record holder at Indy. *Bottom:* Ronnie Householder in the Gerber SO car in 1938—looks like the Cook County Fairgrounds. Householder was primarily a midget driver but did compete at Indy four times. This is a rare dirt track big car appearance. (All photographs—Roy Eaton collection; photographs by Larry Sullivan).

Top: Herschel Buchanan won lots of Midwest races both before and after World War II. He also starred in the stocks late in his career. *Middle:* Bob Sall is in the ex-Gus Schrader 220 Miller at the Cook County Fairgrounds (Chicago) in 1937. Sall won a lot of dirt track races and had one Indy start in 1935. He was a member of the ill prepared Ford team, and—like everybody else—went out with steering box problems. *Bottom:* Buck Whitner spent most of his career on the West Coast but did make several trips to the Midwest. This car was built by owner Leo Krasek who reportedly used metal highway billboard signs to make the body—he might or might not have paid for these! Buck Whitmer was killed at Chico, California, in 1948 (All photographs—Roy Eaton collection; photographs by Larry Sullivan).

Opposite: An IMCA promotional brochure from 1937. While the IMCA was guilty of a bit of hype they were not kidding about the crowds. The state fairs and major county fairs drew huge crowds year after year (Wood collection).

Top right: Glen Coffman and Rajo Jack were both injured in a 1940 crash at Ottumwa, Iowa. Here they are at Des Moines a few days later (Marty Brightman collection). *Bottom:* Howard Wilson, a mechanic for the sponsoring Waldo Motor Service, is shown in the Eaton-Soetaert Ford V-8. The photograph was taken in Kansas City, Missouri, in 1938 (Roy Eaton collection).

Ford V-8

Given the immense popularity of the flathead Ford or Mercury V-8 in the post–World War II track roadsters it is a bit surprising that more V-8s do not show up in late 1930s big car racing. It is doubtful if there are more than a dozen photos of Ford V-8 race cars in this book.

Several factors enter into this lack of V-8s. The late-model engines were no doubt expensive when compared to the Model A, B or T Ford engines that were used as a starting point for many race car engines. Speed equipment for the V-8s existed by the mid 1930s but it was primitive and added little horsepower to a very heavy engine. The main reason was probably the terrible design of the V-8 that made it prone to serious overheating.

Roy Eaton, who now lives in Payette, Idaho, was asked about the V-8-powered big car he owned in 1938. Roy's first words were, "It was a heater!" He quickly added, "It just didn't work out—we wound up replacing it with a Riley two port on a Model A block".

Along with partner Bill Soetaert,

Eaton purchased the car from the Kansas City Ford mechanic who had built it. Other than the fact that the V-8 had two carburetors Roy has forgotten the engine details but he remembers that it sounded great! When Eaton drove the car at Smithville, Missouri, the car was not competitive and overheated badly. Bill Soetaert tried it at Paris, Missouri, with much the same result—maybe even worse, as it was very hot in Paris that day.

Certainly other car owners watched Eaton and Soetaert struggle with the V-8, and stuck with what worked. This pattern was no doubt repeated at many tracks all over the country—the V-8 just never caught on. Starting shortly before World War II the street and dry lake hotrodders would help develop the V-8 into a winning track-roadster engine. In the late 1940s and the 1950s some good flathead V-8 sprint cars were built, but even then most owners stuck with the four-bangers or other proven engines.

Fred Frame

Fred Frame is best remembered as the winner of the 1932 Indianapolis 500. Less known is the fact that Frame preferred the dirt of the county and state fair races. I had the privilege of knowing Fred Frame in the early 1950s, when I was racing sprint cars with the American Racing Association (ARA) in Northern California. Fred was an official with the ARA. A couple of years later I wrote an article on Frame for *Speed Age* and spent a considerable amount of time interviewing him, on various parts of his career. I asked a lot of questions then, but can now think of lots more that I should have asked.

Fred Frame was born in 1895 and his first race came at Southern California's Ascot Park in 1915. A first race doesn't get any less auspicious than Frame's debut. Frame had a near-stock stripped-down Model T; for no good reason, he and mechanic Ed Winfield installed a three-gallon oil tank in the cowl. As the T warmed up for the start the oil drained into the engine and progressively fouled out the spark plugs. The engine spewed out huge clouds of smoke and finally died with a bigger cloud of smoke, as the crowd had a good laugh. Fred Frame admitted he wanted to cry!

Fred Frame at Langhorne on October 17, 1931. Frame won a heat race and the 50-mile feature in this Duesenberg that he drove to a second-place finish at Indy that same year (Haag collection).

It was a AAA race at Santa Maria, in Central California, a few years later that convinced Frame he wanted to be a professional race driver. By this time he was driving a very potent modified Model T. His two main competitors went through the fence on the first lap and this helped Frame get his first win and take home $529. For the next several years Frame built up his reputation on the dirt tracks all across the country. He survived the expected crashes, including a nasty spill at Abilene, Texas, where he got lost in the dust. His first big win was a AAA hundred-miler at Kalamazoo, Michigan, in 1926. Frame was a good businessman and wins like this helped him to command appearance money or hefty guarantees.

Frame first appeared at Indianapolis in 1927. In 1932 he won the big race in the Harry Hartz Miller at a record average of 104.144 MPH.

Right: Fred Frame at Reading, Pennsylvania, in 1932. Frame is driving his own Duesenberg two-man car. That's Frank Farmer on the outside. *Bottom:* Fred Frame leads the way through a dusty turn at Reading in 1932. It is believed that Frame won the feature that day against a field of lighter and more nimble dirt track cars (Both photographs—Haag collection).

The beautiful 183-cubic-inch Fred Frame-built Duesenberg at Indianapolis in 1938. The car was certainly fast enough to make the race, but lack of preparation time doomed the qualifying effort (Joe Gemsa collection).

Frame had two shots at the win that year as Billy Winn drove Frame's Duesenberg to a ninth place finish.

As early as 1927 Fred Frame was campaigning Indy cars in dirt track races. These were AAA-sanctioned races, and some (or most) were promoted by Ralph Hankinson. During the late 1920s and the 1930s Hankinson ran a fair circuit similar to the IMCA promotions. Hankinson's races were mostly in the East; unlike IMCA, they were for-real races and not hippodromes. This didn't prevent Hankinson from paying appearance money to the top drivers. It was probably in 1932 that Fred Frame (with his Indy Duesenberg) was getting $400 just to show up and have a chance at winning another $500.

Frame's last shot at Indy came in 1938 in his own 183-cubic-inch blown Duesenberg. Unfortunately the car was not finished in time for the race, so Frame went outlaw and spent the rest of that summer running the Duesy on the IMCA circuit. He officially retired from racing at the end of 1938, but—like so many—relented, only to be seriously injured practicing for a stock car race at Oakland, California, in 1939.

The Indianapolis Oakland V-8

Among the cars developed for the Indy 500 during the "Junk Formula" era from 1930 to 1936 was an Oakland. The Oakland, a General Motors product and the ancestor of the Pontiac, enjoyed moderate success from its inception in 1908 until the mid 1920s.

In 1929 the company introduced a V-8 engine in an attempt to revive sagging sales. The V-8 was a 251-cubic-inch flathead and rated at 85 horsepower. The engine was a flop, and even though Oakland went to a straight eight in 1933 it was doomed. (The V-8's valve mechanism defies description—the valves were horizontal in the block and activated by rocker arms)

An Oakland, along with a slew of other stock-block machines, was entered in the 1930 Indy race. The car was basically a stripped stock car with a crude racing body. The car was entered by Ira Vail and driven by Clyde Burton in his only Indi-

Ray Hebert in 1931. The Oakland V-8 had a 180-degree crankshaft and was subject to severe vibration (Wood collection).

anapolis appearance. There is no evidence of factory support. Burton qualified the car at 95.097 MPH, some 18 MPH off pole-winner Billy Arnold's pace, but not the slowest in the field. In the race Burton got credit for 11th place when he was flagged after 197 laps.

Over the years a few of the Oakland V-8s showed up in dirt track cars. One of these was in South Dakota and Iowa in 1931 and this car might have been fairly successful. It was a nice-looking car and one of the better drivers was behind the wheel — Ray Hebert. The car was billed as the "Indianapolis Oakland 8"; given the climate of the times, there is little doubt that the car would be billed by publicists as having raced at Indianapolis. Maybe the Indy car was cut down to a one-man configuration? It would be nice if this were true but, unfortunately it is not.

A comparison of an excellent picture of the Indy car with the photo above just does not check out. Is it the Indy engine? Who knows? Let's give Ray Hebert the benefit of the doubt.

7

Lake States
Michigan, Indiana, Ohio

There was lots of between-the-wars racing in these three states, and by comparison to other areas it reasonably well documented.

Michigan had racing as early as 1899 on a mile oval at the State Fairgrounds in Detroit. This track also hosted the first-ever IMCA race on May 30, 1915. There was pre–World War I racing at cities like Grand Rapids, Kalamazoo and Grosse Point near Detroit. Henry Ford started and finished his career as a driver at Grosse Point: in 1901 he won the only race he ever drove. In the 1920s and '30s racing continued at the State Fairgrounds in Detroit and went on until 1966 when the race track became a parking lot. Detroit also had racing at the V.F.W. Speedway. At Grand Rapids racing took place from 1903 until 1937 on a mile-and-one-eighth somewhat lopsided oval.

Kalamazoo had a mile track that was active from 1914 to 1935, while in Jackson there was racing at the fairgrounds from 1913 to 1937 and then

Fred Horey and Ben Giroux (aka Ben Gotoff) graced the cover of this program for an IMCA race at an unknown location—probably about 1920 (Saal collection).

again in 1941 and 1942. Ann Arbor while known for a certain football team, had racing in the 1930s. Other Michigan cities that had racing include Mount Clemens, Dawson, Cadillac, East Lansing and Fowlerville—Ralph Hepburn raced motorcycles here in 1926. Further north, the only known racing on Michigan's Upper Peninsula was at Escanaba from 1928 to 1941 and at Iron Mountain in 1941.

There was a bit of 1920s and '30s racing in Indiana—somehow, this is not surprising. Allan Brown's *History of America's Speedways* lists a mere 64 tracks that had big-car racing from 1919 to 1941. Racing started at the Fort Wayne Driving Park in 1902. At the State Fairgrounds in Indianapolis racing got underway in 1903 and is still going on. Indianapolis Motor Speedway started as a dirt track in 1909, but this didn't work out and they paved the place. Winchester opened in 1914 as a flat oiled dirt oval, was banked in 1922, and additional banking was added in 1929. This track was oiled dirt until 1950. Another well-known speedway, Jungle Park, opened in 1926 with semi-paved straights and dirt corners. Roby Speedway is often thought

Right: Ben Gotoff in his Miller someplace in Ohio in 1922. This may be the Barney Oldfield car that finished last in the 1919 Indy race with Roscoe Sarles at the wheel. Note the similarity of the nose to Barney's famous "Golden Submarine." Also, the color appears to be the same. *Below:* Check this refueling rig! Probably an IMCA show around 1920 (Both photographs—Saal collection).

Top: An unknown driver in an unknown car at an unknown track—ca. 1920. *Bottom:* This machine appears a bit battered, but judging by the exhaust pipe, it must be a Duesenberg (Both photographs—Don Moore collection).

of as being in Chicago, but it was just over the state line in Hammond, Indiana. This one-mile dirt oval operated from 1920 to 1936. Terre Haute had racing on several tracks but none were really successful until the present Action Track was built in 1949. In Salem it was more or less the same story—several tracks ran in the area but only intermittently. Other tracks that appear on the Indiana list include Crown Point, South Bend, Hammond, Lafayette, Burlington and the oddly-named Black Demon Speedway northwest of Terre Haute.

Ohio had some of the earliest racing in the nation at the Glenville Driving Track near Cleveland on May 30, 1897. Columbus and Toledo had racing shortly after the turn of the century. After the First World War Cleveland had racing at four tracks—

Top: Roby Speedway, September 23, 1923. Al Karp is on the pole, Sam Davis is in #999, and #14 is Esthan Wemester. Roby was located in Hammond, Indiana, and served the Chicago area (Murawski collection). *Bottom:* Leo Young in a typical Model T Ford–based race car of the mid-1920s. Absolutely nothing is known about Leo Young—another forgotten race driver (Christine Horey Logan collection from Grace Jones).

Brookpark, Randall Park, Thistledowns and a half-mile track whose name has been forgotten. Cincinnati had only two tracks: the Cincinnati-Hamilton Speedway ran from 1929 to 1941, and there was a short-lived track at the Hamilton Fairgrounds in 1936. In Columbus the Columbus Driving Park operated up to 1925 and there was also racing at Beulah Park and at the Ohio State Fairgrounds. Dayton had intermittent racing at the Montgomery County Fairgrounds until Dayton Speedway opened in 1934. It started as a flat five-eighths-mile square track and became a high-banked half-miler in 1939. Fort Miami Speedway, near Toledo, had racing form 1918 to 1942. Among other Ohio cities that had big-car racing were New Bremen, Sandusky, Canton and (from 1929 to 1942) Sharon Speedway—this was in Ohio but named after Sharon, Pennsylvania.

Top: This, according to the original photograph caption, is a "Factory Fronty Ford." No ID on the driver—the date is around 1925 (Harold Osmer collection). *Bottom:* Sonny Talament in his own Rajo T at Roby in 1926. Look at that crowd! Roby was a successful operation from about 1920 to 1937 when the grandstands were condemned (Emil Andres collection).

Top: Wilbur Shaw at Roby in 1927. The car is the same Miller "Whippet Special" that Shaw drove at Daytona Beach in an attempt to set a four-cylinder speed record. The car caught on fire and Shaw had to douse the flames by driving into the Atlantic Ocean (Murawski collection). *Right:* J. Alex Sloan was great showman in his own right but he sometimes imported the greatest racing showman of all time to help hype an event—Barney Oldfield. *Left:* J. Alex Sloan was one of the great promoters of the 1920s and 1930s. He promoted hundreds of events and most of these were under the sanction of the International Motor Contest Association. Sloan was *Mister* IMCA (Lower photographs—Christine Horey Logan collection from Grace Jones).

Top: Records indicate that most of the races at Roby Speedway were under AAA sanction. Here is Jack Petticord in 1927 at Roby with the same car he drove at Indy that year (Murawski collection). *Middle:* Vernon McCombs in the Lasham Special someplace in Indiana in 1929. McCombs died in a crash at Marion, Ohio, on July 12, 1936—tragically, just one day after his baby daughter was born. *Bottom:* Ernie Triplett in 1927. Triplett was born in the Midwest and started his racing career there. Most of his fame came from winning the race at Legion Ascot Speedway in Los Angeles (Lower photographs—Roy Eaton collection; photographs by Larry Sullivan).

Top: Lou Schneider won the 1931 Indianapolis 500. Here he is at a dirt-track race probably in about 1930 (Christine Horey Logan Collection from Grace Jones). *Middle:* Little is known about this photograph. It was probably taken at Detroit and this may be the same car Chet Miller drove to a 17th place finish at Indy in 1930 (Jim Way collection). *Bottom:* Shorty Cantlon at Detroit in 1931. His Bowe's Seal Fast Special has an Art Chevrolet-designed stagger-valve T-based engine — a double-overhead-valve head with two intake and three exhaust ports on each side (Roy Eaton collection; photograph by Larry Sullivan).

Top: This is Detroit or Milwaukee in 1930. The car is the Russ Snowberger Studebaker Eight that he drove to an eighth-place finish at Indianapolis in that same year. The 336-cubic-inch Studebaker pushed this ungainly-looking machine to a qualifying speed of 104.166 MPH at Indy. *Middle:* Frank Brisco in 1932. Brisco was a fine dirt track driver and had 13 appearances at Indy. Brisco also developed his own six-cylinder DOHC engines that ran at Indy shortly before the war (Emil Andres collection). *Bottom:* This is Wilbur Shaw in 1931 at either Detroit or Milwaukee. The two-man Indy cars were run on one-mile dirt tracks at National Championship events. Riding mechanics were not required on the dirt (Top and bottom photographs—Osmer collection).

Top: Howdy Wilcox is shown in the Chevrolet stagger-valve Fronty in 1931. That's designer Art Chevrolet in the hat and tie. Chevrolet built only about six of these stagger-valve heads for the Model T. All the cars fitted with them ran fast (Roy Eaton collection; photograph by Larry Sullivan). *Middle:* Doc MacKenzie was one of the best drivers of the early 1930s. He competed at Indy from 1930 to 1936 and posted a third-place finish in 1936. He won the AAA Eastern Championship in 1935. This popular driver was killed at Milwaukee on August 23, 1936 (Osmer collection). *Bottom:* A huge crowd is on hand to see the Indy cars run on the dirt at Detroit on June 14, 1931. Car #15 is probably driven by Bert Karnatz who did not qualify at Indy, and #21 should be Myron Stevens who finished fourth at Indy in 1931 (Jim Haag collection; photograph by Kirkpatrick).

Top: Johnny Wohlfeil in the mid–1930s. Wohlfeil had a long and successful career driving both big cars and midgets in the Detroit area. In 1936 he took an outboard midget to North Carolina and beat the big cars (Osmer collection). *Middle:* Emil Andres at an unknown track in about 1935. Andres raced for many years and was a winner in both the midgets and big cars. He ran at Indy from 1935 to 1950, with his best finish a fourth place in 1946. Andres was a respected racing historian until his death in 1999 (Osmer collection; photograph by Ed Hitze). *Bottom:* Billy Winn at Detroit in 1936. Winn was one of the real greats in Midwestern and Eastern racing. He was at Indianapolis from 1931 to 1938, with his best performance a ninth place in 1932. Winn was killed on August 20, 1938, at Springfield, Illinois (Emil Andres collection).

Top: Mauri Rose at an unknown Midwestern track in about 1936. Rose's exploits at Indianapolis are legend, but he was also a fine dirt-track racer in his earlier days. Rose is getting set to drive the Lou Moore Miller (Emil Andres collection). *Right:* Fritz Tegtmeier at Milwaukee in 1937. This may be a AAA race, but Tegtmeier spent most of his career with the IMCA and was still active in the mid–1950s (Ray Eaton collection; photograph by Larry Sullivan). *Left:* This is a photograph of Shorty Drexler and Buddy Callaway in the mid–1930s. We can probably guess which is which (Christine Horey Logan collection from Grace Jones).

Top: Louie Unser is famous for winning a bunch of Pikes Peak races, but he also drove in some oval-track events. He is shown in the Russ Snowberger Miller at Milwaukee in 1937 (Roy Eaton collection; photograph by Larry Sullivan). *Middle:* The field lines up at Winchester in about 1940. Winchester was not the fine track it is today. The surface was oiled dirt and the crash wall was made of water pipe—a very hazardous place! *Bottom:* A lineup at Fort Wayne in 1940. Note the lack of a crash wall on those high banks—just a dirt beam to act as a launching ramp into the trees. At least seven drivers died at Fort Wayne over the years (Lower photographs—Osmer collection).

Top: A fine action shot at Winchester. No identification on the drivers—it may be a AAA race or an outlaw event (Osmer collection; photograph by Ed Hitze). *Middle:* Elbert "Pappy" Booker at Dayton in about 1940. Booker competed on the high banks of the Midwest for many years. He won the 1946 AAA Midwestern Championship but was killed the following year at Dayton (Osmer collection). *Bottom:* Jimmy Wilburn at Winchester in about 1940. There may be a 318-cubic-inch Offy under the hood of the Riverside Tires machine. Note the minimal protection for the spectators (Joe Gemsa collection).

Top: Windy Jennings drove this nice-looking Riley in Midwestern races (Osmer collection). *Middle:* Billy McGee in the Herm Wilson Riley at Painsville, Illinois, in 1941. Although not a big winner McGee drove in a lot of AAA races. To McGee went the dubious distinction of finishing the race in the car that Hal Cole started at Del Mar, California, in 1949—the machine that had killed Rex Mays. *Bottom:* Bob Paul managed a weak smile after surviving a nasty-looking flip at Sharon Speedway. Although named after nearby Sharon, Pennsylvania, the race track was in Ohio (Middle and bottom photographs—Saal collection; photographs by Brownie).

Opposite top: Ray Courtney someplace in Ohio. This Studebaker Straight Eight machine was described as "a foul-handling pig." In the 1930s the

Studebaker Corporation sold racing engines for $750—odds are this is one of them (Saal collection; photograph by Brownie). *Middle:* Woody Woodford is shown at Winchester in 1940. Originally from the Pacific Northwest, Woodford moved to the Midwest so he could complete in more races. He died in a Greenville, Ohio, crash in 1942—a crash that also took the life of Zook Harton (Osmer collection; photograph by Ed Hitze). *Bottom:* Everett Saylor at Jungle Park. Most of Saylor's early career was spent in the Central States Racing Association (CSRA), but he quit the outlaw group to run with the AAA hoping for a shot at Indy. Saylor had an Indy ride in 1941 but crashed late in the event. Saylor died at dusty Cape Girardeau, Missouri, on May 31, 1942 (Osmer collection).

Top: Pete Alberts in the Hank O'Day Offy. Alberts ran into problems with the law, and for a time, drove under the name of Pietro Alberti—not a very clever alias but it apparently worked. Alberts was killed at Mt. Vernon, Illinois, on September 17, 1939. *Middle:* Les Adair at Jungle Park in around 1940. Adair usually ran with outlaw groups. When racing with the AAA, he went by the names Les Mundy or Babe Brown. He was fatally injured at Franklin, Indiana, in 1948 (Top and middle photographs—Osmer collection). *Bottom:* Travis "Spider" Webb at Milwaukee in 1941. Webb primarily drove on the dirt prior to World War II but had six Indianapolis starts after the war. Mechanical problems kept him from any top finishes (Roy Eaton collection; photograph by Larry Sullivan).

Top: Joie Chitwood is shown at Milwaukee in 1941. Although better known for his thrill show exploits, Chitwood was a winning driver in races all over the eastern half of the United States. In seven Indy starts he had three fifth-place finishes to his credit (Roy Eaton collection; photograph Larry Sullivan). *Middle:* Close action at Norwalk, Ohio, in 1940. Earl Harton is in #6 and that may be Chuck Rice on the outside. The Norwalk track, at the Huron County Fairgrounds, held races from 1923 to 1948. *Bottom:* Main event action at Powell, Ohio, in 1941. Red Bales is in #39 and the #505 is one of the Merkler Hissos. This track ran from June of 1939 to 1941. Later on there were four different tracks at the same site and racing continued until 1965 (Lower photographs—Saal collection; photographs by Brownie).

Top: The lineup at South Bend, Indiana—probably in 1942. Most likely this is a CSRA event and that should be Windy Jennings in #5. The track looks a bit run-down—not unusual in those days (Osmer collection). *Bottom:* Tommy Legge was from the Pacific Northwest and starred in the midgets in that area. In 1941 he traveled to the Midwest to race big cars and is pictured at Fort Wayne, Indiana. Legge died later that year in a Dayton crash (Bill Hill collection).

Ben Gotoff

Ben Gotoff was a capable race driver who, like so many, has been all but forgotten in history. Gotoff raced with the IMCA from about 1915 to 1922 and competed throughout the Midwest from Louisiana to Canada. At some point, probably late in his life, he compiled a scrapbook–photo album of his racing career. Tom Saal made copies of this and Ben Gotoff will not be completely forgotten.

In a way the Gotoff clippings and photos ask more questions than they answer. Most photos were not identified. The press clippings were not dated, nor did most include the newspaper name and location. There are references in the text of the clippings to "the Fairgrounds," "this city" and "locally." Where on earth were

DAVE KOETZLA of Detroit, Mich.
Who bears the distinction of being the World's youngest record holding professional race driver

"Texas" George Clark at the wheel of his Record Holding Case

BEN GIROUX Foreign Driver
Winner of the Moscow-Odessa Road Race
also other important European Dirt Track and Road Events

8 Champion Professional Automobile Race Drivers

$2000 IN PRIZES

$2000 IN PRIZES

Ben Giroux, Great European Auto Race Driver who defeated many of America's Greatest Stars

Ben Gotoff, or "Ben Giroux" at J. Alex Sloan's option, was a star IMCA driver preceding Fred Horey and Sig Haugdahl. These circa 1918 newspaper ads are full of the hype that typified a Sloan promotion. The "Moscow-Odessa Road Race" almost certainly never happened (There were a few pre–World War I races in Russia, but an event of over 700 miles seems a bit much.) Odds are Sloan just picked out two cities on the map of Russia and declared "Giroux" the winner. One also has to wonder about the "$2000 in Prizes." At the time Sloan's drivers were probably on salaries of $50 to $100 per week, and there was no prize money (Saal collection).

these places? Frustrating, but nonetheless valuable to the historian. Surfacing in this material was the information that there was night racing in Akron, Ohio, in about 1916. They used carbide lamps to illuminate the track!

Nobody knows where or when Ben Gotoff was born or when he died. He might have been born in Europe, and there is a remote possibility that he raced there. This theory requires believing some IMCA publicity put out by J. Alex Sloan—we all know racing promoters *never* lie. Sloan took advantage of Gotoff's European (?) background to rename him "Ben Giroux" whenever he wanted a foreign driver in the field. (This predates Sloan's turning George Stewart into Leon Duray).

Gotoff started racing in a National. Later on he drove a Sunbeam-Isotta and in the early 1920s piloted one of the first cars that Harry Miller built. Gotoff was a winner and an advertised feature driver. He did his share of crashing, and, from photos of the remains of some of these cars, was lucky to survive. It is believed he quit racing in 1922 while still a relatively young man—family obligations might have had something to do with this.

(Thanks to Tom Saal of Lakewood, Ohio, for Ben Gotoff information and photographs.)

Hammond and the Rim Riders

Meaner than a junkyard dog? How about meaner than a junkyard race track? The track at Hammond, Indiana, was a mean place. Built in a combination garbage

Les Duncan is on the way over the rim at Hammond. Will he land in the swampy lake, or the junkyard? What a choice! (Sowle collection).

Top: Action at Hammond in 1938 or 1939 as Bayliss Levrett runs third in #91. Note that the photographer is standing on rubble and garbage. *Bottom:* Levrett's own words describe what happened to him at Hammond. He escaped with minor injuries (Both photographs—John Levrett collection).

The Bayliss Levrett car burns at Hammond (John Levrett collection).

dump and junkyard, Hammond was the scene of some spectacular racing—and spectacular accidents—in the years just before World War II.

The track was in an industrial area on the outskirts of Chicago and popular with fans from that city. It was a five-eighths-mile, semi-banked oiled dirt oval. The track builders apparently dug a hole to get some clean dirt to construct the track—this left a swampy lake on the outside of one turn. Outside the other turn was assorted construction rubble and old cars. These potential landing places might be acceptable if the crash wall would normally keep a car on the speedway. At Hammond, the "crash wall" appears to be nothing more than a bulldozed pile of rubble and garbage that launched cars into space.

Hammond operated, probably mostly under CSRA sanction, from 1937 to mid–1942 and for a short period after the war. Advertisements proclaimed the drivers who raced at Hammond as "The Rim Riders." They had to be brave men. In only a relatively few races Hammond took the lives of Leonard Powell and Buzz Mendenhall.

Henry Meyer

Henry Meyer is best remembered as a car owner and a top-notch mechanic for the famed Iddings Specials. The lesser-known part of Meyer's racing career was before World War II, and much of this was behind the wheel of dirt track cars all over the eastern part of the US.

Meyer's long involvement in racing began in 1927 when he and a friend purchased a very wrecked Fronty Ford racer. Meyer worked for months putting the car in shape to race and made his debut as a driver in 1928. It turned out that 1928 was a good year by Henry's standards—no broken bones and the car in one piece. To say that Henry Meyer was a hard charger is an understatement—he was on the gas at all times. He won some big races, like a hundred-miler at Cantfield, Ohio but the inevitable crashes resulted in major injuries. He was even pronounced dead after a spill at Columbus, Ohio.

With the advent of the midgets in the mid–1930s, Meyer turned most of his attention to the small cars and took his last big car ride in 1936. Henry won races

Top: Henry Meyer is shown in the Wright Brothers Fronty at New Bremen, Ohio, in 1932. Meyer campaigned the tough dirt tracks of Ohio and Indiana where his heavy foot helped him win races—and trips to the hospital. *Bottom:* The beautiful Fronty restored by Henry Meyer is shown at the Latimore Valley Fairgrounds in Pennsylvania, home of the Eastern Museum of Motor Racing (Both photographs—Bob and Judy Moore collection).

in a Saxton and in Harley-powered cars. A 1939 midget crash at Hershey, Pennsylvania, put an end to his driving career.

Henry Meyer's second career in racing began in 1938 when he, along with his brother Bob and friend Bob Moore, constructed the Iddings Hal. This car had a long winning record in both CSRA and AAA sprint car events. In 1948, Meyer stretched the car to Indy specs and Lee Wallard drove it to an amazing seventh-place finish. Henry Meyer remained in close contact with John and Howard Iddings and their race cars until the early 1970s. In the 1980s he was active in restoring both cars and engines. In 1990 a long-cherished dream for Henry came true when he completed a total restoration of a 1928 Fronty Ford—a twin to the car that started him on a lifelong love affair with auto racing. He died of cancer in 1994 at the age of 86.

Larry Sullivan

Above all, Larry Sullivan was a race fan. He took some 5,000 photographs that spanned racing history from Gus Schrader in 1927 to Steve Kinser in the 19902, but he was not a professional photographer—he was just a fan.

Most of Larry Sullivan's photos were taken with a simple and inexpensive Kodak box camera. His photos were posed car and driver shots—images that preserved chunks of racing history at scores of little-known outlaw race tracks in the Midwest. Larry also wrote about racing for a half-dozen publications, and his "Midwest Whispers" in *National Speed Sport News* was a must for big car fans for many years. He richly deserved the honor of being inducted into the Sprint Car Hall of Fame in 1999. Larry passed away in the spring of 2000.

There are a couple of dozen known Larry Sullivan photos in this book and perhaps some others that are his work, but the photographer's credits have been lost over the years.

Thank you, Larry Sullivan, for being such a devoted racing fan.

Mount Clemens

Very little is known about Mount Clemens Race Track. It was a horse track, and it is recorded that races were held there in 1920 and 1936. These rare photos show racing at Mount Clemens in 1923. The year can be verified

Above and opposite: Six cars from 1923 at Mount Clemens (All photographs—Harold Osmer collection).

by auto license plates and the fact that an advertised racing date of Sunday July 29 checks out with a 1923 calendar.

The cars are unusual in that they are not the bobtails common in 1923 but do have full racing bodies. The very low car has the driver seated alongside the driveshaft—a forerunner of the Indy roadsters of the 1950s. It is a shame that the names of the men appearing in the photos have been forgotten.

Mount Clemens is located about 15 miles north of Detroit. Races were held at the site of the original speedway until 1972.

The New Bremen Riot

As with any sport, auto racing is subject to occasional disagreements, arguments, and out-and-out fistfights. What happened at New Bremen, Ohio on September 20, 1931, was almost a major disaster and probably ranks as the worst riot in racing history.

There was a huge crowd on hand at New Bremen Speedway on that Sunday afternoon and everything went smoothly until it was time for the feature race. Apparently the drivers had signed entry blanks calling for a purse of $525 for the race, but when they lined up on the track they demanded that the purse be $750. Perhaps the huge crowd had something to do with this demand, which was quickly refused by the track management. A long delay ensued as the argument got louder and louder—the fact that the public address system was inadvertently left open and the angry words of both sides were broadcast to the crowd did not help matters. At this point most of the drivers abandoned their cars and moved to the grandstands where they acted as cheerleaders for the chant, "Start the race! Start the race!"

A thrown pop bottle set off the now-furious crowd which promptly became an uncontrolled mob. Part of the mob charged to the infield where, by brute force, they pulled down the official's stand. Race officials scrambled to safety amid a shower of pop bottles and seats from the grandstands. Gasoline from the pits was poured on the official's stand and on the grandstands and soon both were ablaze. The ugly crowd threatened anybody who tried to fight the flames. The mélée went on into the night until the rioters were finally quelled by law enforcement officers. By then the speedway grounds were in ruin.

News reports make no mention of a sanctioning body so maybe there was none, but some well-known drivers were on hand. The starting field for the ill-fated feature included Howdy Wilcox, Bob Carey, Bill Chitum, Clay Corbitt and Al Miller.

VFW Speedway

This track, also known as Motor City Speedway, operated from October 2, 1932, until late in 1938. The slightly-banked half-mile oiled dirt track was located

Top: Everett Saylor. *Bottom:* Paul Zimmer (Both photographs—Harold Osmer collection).

Top: Outside, future Indy star Henry Banks. Inside, Campie Franazo. *Middle:* Howard Dauphin. *Bottom:* Unknown. (All photographs—Harold Osmer collection)

on Eight Mile Road not too far from downtown Detroit. The track opened under AAA sanction and Bob Carey was the first feature winner. The AAA sanction continued in 1933 and Mauri Rose posted a main-event win. After that VFW Speedway went to open competition, and the names of most of the drivers are not too familiar. Some of the better-known drivers of the Central States Racing Association (CSRA) made occasional appearances. The track's demise in 1938 can be blamed on the midgets, as a quarter-miler replaced the bigger track. Several midget, and later stock car, tracks ran at the same site until 1958.

Thanks to Harold Osmer of Los Angeles, excellent photos of VFW Speedway are available. Osmer is a racing historian and the author of two fine books—*Where They Raced* and *Real Road Racing*. Unfortunately, it is not known who took the remarkably clear photographs from VFW Speedway. The exact dates are unknown but all are probably between 1934 and 1938.

Top: Unknown. *Opposite middle:* Vern Frank. *Opposite bottom:* Johnny Wohlfiel, Mel Moore Hisso (All photographs—Harold Osmer collection)

8

Northeast

Maine, New Hampshire, Vermont, New York, Massachusetts, Connecticut, Rhode Island

Maine had but half a dozen tracks that operated before World War II. Beach races were held at Old Orchard Beach from about 1911 to 1916. It would be almost 20 years before another race was held in Maine—this at the Topsham Fairgrounds

This photograph was probably taken at South Attleboro, Massachusetts, in about 1925. If so, this is the Interstate Speedway Park which held intermittent races from 1922 to 1938. The driver is unknown (Bob Silvia collection).

8. Northeast (ME, NH, VT, NY, MA, CT, RI)

This is a two-man Terraplane built by Johnny Whitehouse. Probably about 1930 and in Connecticut (Joe Fiore collection).

near Brunswick on October 27, 1935. Kennebunk had racing on July 4, 1936, and there was a race on a mile-and-one-eighth oval at Old Orchard in about 1937. Lewiston and North Gloucester had a bit of racing around 1940.

In New Hampshire things got underway at Rockingham Speedway in Salem in 1912 with races on a one-mile track. This was the same site as Rockingham Motor Speedway, the high-banked board track that ran in the mid–1920s. After the demise of the board track, races were held on the dirt in 1931—oddly enough, the IMCA ventured this far east for a race on October 12, 1931. Elsewhere in New Hampshire there was speedway action at Newmarket starting in 1927 and at Keene beginning in 1935. The Granite State Park Speedway at Dover ran intermittent races a mile and a half-mile track from 1934 to 1942. At Canobie Lake there was a dirt oval at an amusement park that ran races either in the 1910s or the 1920s. Hannahan Farm near West Swansey ran two races in 1940.

There was no known racing in Vermont until September 8, 1928, when a AAA race was held on the half-mile oval at the state fairgrounds in Rutland. This track held occasional races until 1941. Essex Junction saw racing in 1932 and then again from about 1939 to 1941. Ira Vail was the promoter at this track. A few races at Burgess Field near Bennington, at Huntington and at Morrisville complete the rather meager history of prewar racing in Vermont.

New York had lots of racing and much of it was before World War I. The road courses, such as those on Long Island, are better known but there were also some

Top: Frank Alden gets ready to be pulled off at Newmarket, New Hampshire, in 1930. This former horse track was active from 1927 to 1942 and might have run one race after World War II (Bob Silvia collection). *Middle:* Bill Mitchell drove this nice-looking car on New York dirt tracks around 1930 (Joe Fiore collection). *Bottom:* Bub Walker of Lawrenceville New York, smiles after a dusty race. Walker competed in Pennsylvania as well as in New York (Jim Way collection).

Top: October 7, 1934, at Dover, New Hampshire, and Bob King gets ready to go. This is the Granite State Park Speedway—a one-mile horse track that ran a few races between 1934 and 1941. It was replaced by half-mile oval that lasted until 1948. *Middle:* Nothing is known about this photograph other than that it was taken in New England in 1935 (Joe Fiore collection). *Bottom*: Everett Morrisette drove this nice-looking car on New England tracks in the late 1930s (Top and bottom photographs—Bob Silvia collection).

dirt ovals. Tracks at Buffalo, Binghamton, Syracuse and Rochester all hosted some early races. Rochester had racing as early as 1898. The New York State Fairgrounds at Syracuse saw racing begin in 1909 and it is still going on today. One of the nation's finest drivers, Jimmy Murphy, was fatally injured here on September 15, 1924. Some of the better-known New York tracks were located at Altamont, Caledonia, Deer Park, Dunkirk, Fonda, Middletown, Rhinebeck, and Watertown. Lesser-known tracks operated at dozens of county fairgrounds.

New York City had a remarkable amount of racing considering its population density. Manhattan had midget racing on several ovals but no big cars. In the Bronx a one-mile track at Morris Park operated from 1905 to 1907. Queens had racing at Crossbay from 1934 to 1939, at Holmes Airport Speedway and at the Maspeth Fairgrounds. The Maspeth track, located near Metropolitan Heights, was active from 1927 to 1929. Holmes Airport at Jackson Heights ran in 1932. The Brooklyn racing was at Brighton Beach, just east of Coney Island, on a one-mile track from 1902 to about 1915, and at a dirt track on Sheepshead Bay in 1910. (This was the site of the two-mile board track from 1915 to 1920). On Staten Island the Bray Brook Oval held races on unknown dates.

The first race in Massachusetts was at Charles River Park, Cambridge, in November of 1898. A Stanley Steamer won the race on a one-third-mile oval. Readville, near Boston at Hyde Park, got going in 1902 and operated with both

Mike Fiore is shown someplace in New England in about 1934. The bodywork is a bit rough but this was typical of many of the home built cars of this era (Jim Way collection).

IMCA and AAA events until 1937. In Brockton the Brockton Fairgrounds had a half-mile oval that was active from the early 1920s to 1941 — there were a reported 94,000 fans on hand for a 1934 AAA race. The Eastern States Expo Speedway at West Springfield was another well used track and ran from 1917 until 1941. Among other Massachusetts speedways were Athol, New Bedford, Lakeville, Marshfield, Northhampton, Weymouth and Worcester.

Connecticut racing began at Bedford Park in New Haven on July 25, 1899. The Danbury Fair started holding racing in 1905 on a half-mile dirt track and this continued until 1939. Charter Oak Park in Hartford held races on a mile oval from 1905 to 1920 — races on a half-mile track continued intermittently in the 1920s. Other dirt tracks were located at Bristol, Avon, Sheldon, Rockville, Windsor and Norwich.

Right: Ace Lewis sends fence posts flying at Keene, New Hampshire, in 1936. This is the Safford Park Fairgrounds where a half-mile oval was active from 1935 to about 1961. *Bottom:* The big cars get ready for warm-ups at Middletown, New York. The half-miler at the Orange County Fairgrounds ran from 1919 to 1967, and a five-eighths-mile oval at the same site is still running today (Both photographs — Jim Way collection).

Thompson Speedway is no doubt Connecticut's best-known track—it opened in 1940 but was a paved oval.

Rhode Island, despite its small size, had big car racing at four locations. To Rhode Island goes the distinction of holding the first race on a race track in the United States. This was at Narragansett Park in Cranston on a one-mile horse track. The date was September 7, 1896, and Harry Morris was the winner. A few days later 50,000 people showed up for a race at the same track. This track held races until 1913, and in 1915 a banked asphalt oval was built that operated until 1923. At the Newport Fairground races took place from 1900 to 1904, with a few events in 1937, 1940 and 1941. Pascoag had a half-miler that ran from 1938 to 1940—a 1950 race here may have been the last big car race held in the state. The other Rhode Island dirt oval was at the Woonsocket Fairgrounds—a race was held here on November 2, 1924.

Left: Joe Bob is shown at Crossbay Speedway on Long Island in 1936. Bob was a winner in both the big cars and midgets. He died in a 1937 big car crash at Bird-In-Hand, Pennsylvania (Jim Way collection). *Bottom:* Sim Clark in 1938—probably Altamont, New York. Clark was a well-known midget owner in California in the 1950s and '60s. His midgets won several Bay Cities Racing Association championships and racked up victories in USAC events. Reportedly, Clark's first midget used body parts off this big car (Jack Earle collection).

Top: George Canapwa wheels the Sim Clark machine around an unknown New York track. *Middle:* Chief Sun Hawk was one of the few Native Americans who competed in racing. This photograph was taken at a New England track in about 1938. It appears that #4 has a Ford V-8 engine (Top and middle photographs—Jim Way collection). *Bottom:* The Central States Racing Association was a long way from home in Brockton, Massachusetts, in 1937. Here Jackie Holmes chases Bayliss Levrett in the #36 Hal (Levrett collection).

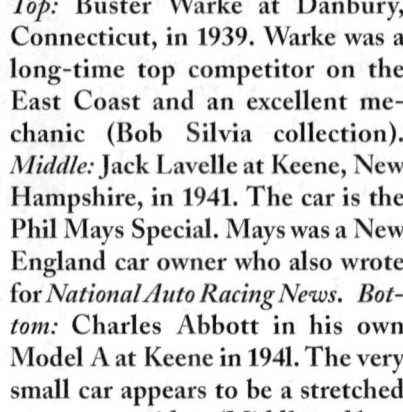

Top: Buster Warke at Danbury, Connecticut, in 1939. Warke was a long-time top competitor on the East Coast and an excellent mechanic (Bob Silvia collection). *Middle:* Jack Lavelle at Keene, New Hampshire, in 1941. The car is the Phil Mays Special. Mays was a New England car owner who also wrote for *National Auto Racing News*. *Bottom:* Charles Abbott in his own Model A at Keene in 1941. The very small car appears to be a stretched midget (Middle and bottom photographs—Jim Way collection).

8. *Northeast* (ME, NH, VT, NY, MA, CT, RI) 197

Top: That's Harold Shaw on the outside and West Coast ace Bud Rose in #3. This is Brockton, Massachusetts, in 1940—almost certainly an IMCA event (Jim Way collection). *Bottom:* Brockton in 1940 as Johnny Nowles leads Shorty Drexler. There is no dust, but that outside fence looks a bit hazardous (Bob Silvia collection).

Top: The field gets ready for warmups at Huntington Speedway, Sheldon, Connecticut, in about 1939. This half-mile oval operated from around 1933 to 1939. *Bottom:* An unknown driver at an unknown track. The nice-looking Rosemary Special has a polished aluminum body—unusual and a lot of work to build (Both photographs—Bob Silvia collection).

Top: Joe Sostillio kicks up a cloud of dust at Weymouth, Massachusetts as spectators crowd the inside rail. It is easy to see why accidents involving fans were almost common. Sostillio starred in both the big cars and midgets and had a shot at Indy in 1953. *Bottom left:* A car roars down the narrow front straight at Keene, New Hampshire. As indicated in some of the photographs, crowd control was a bit lax at some New England tracks. Note the toddler sitting on the ground under the rail (Top and bottom left photographs—Bob Silvia collection). *Bottom right:* George Manley knocks down some fence at Middletown, N.Y., in 1941. From the looks of the background perhaps Manley got lost in the dust (Bob Silvia collection; photograph by Frank Loutiel).

Top: Howard "Bumpy" Bumpus at Thompson Speedway in 1941. This Connecticut oval was one of the first paved big car tracks in the East. Bumpus won the 1941 New England–Eastern States championship in this DO Hal. He died in a 1946 crash at Flemington, N.J (Fiore collection). *Middle:* Louie Giullano drove this nice-looking Cragar at Thompson Speedway in 1941. Note the tension rod under the frame—this probably didn't do much to stiffen what look like Model T frame rails (Bob Silvia collection). *Bottom:* Andy Dunlop is shown with driver Jimmy Canino at Syracuse, New York, in 1939. Dunlop had a long career owning and wrenching cars from the prewar dirt track era to Indy after the war (Dunlop collection).

Top: This looks like Readville, Massachusetts. Eddie Staneck is the driver, and that sure is a slick-looking logo on the cowl of the car. *Middle:* A nice action shot at a New England track in the late 1930s. With cable fences racing was hazardous—so was watching a race (Top and middle photographs—Joe Freeman collection from Bob Silvia). *Bottom:* A fine photograph of action at Readville Speedway, near Boston, in 1936. Eddie Staneck leads Ernie Gessell. This one-mile oval operated from 1902 until 1937. It was a dangerous place where at least three drivers died between 1926 and 1936 (Bob Silvia collection).

Bronco Bill

Bronco Bill Schindler was a remarkable race driver and a remarkable man. He started his career in sports competition as a prizefighter. Bill Schindler admitted he was not a remarkable prizefighter, "I always wound up looking worse than the guy I beat!"

Schindler began racing in 1931 on a Class B big car circuit in Indiana. He enjoyed only moderate success until the midgets came along in 1934. With midget racing flourishing on the East Coast Schindler moved to Freeport, Long Island to be near the center of the action. He drove midgets five or six nights a week and the big cars on Sundays. (It is probably here that Schindler acquired the nickname of "Bronco Bill"—a rough rider.) A turning point in Bill Schindler's career and life came at Mineola, Long Island, in the summer of 1936. Schindler cut it a bit too close in a big car race and tangled with the fence. One of the deadly boards from the fence mangled his left leg so badly it had to be amputated just above the knee.

A crash like that would stop most drivers, but it only seemed to inspire Bill Schindler. He came out of the hospital to win an indoor midget championship in the winter of 1936-37. From then until World War II he won scores of midget races and ran up front in the big cars.

When racing resumed in late 1945, Bill Schindler cashed in on the heyday of midget racing. His record of 106 feature wins in the two years of 1946 and 1947 will never be surpassed. Those were the days when there was racing six or seven nights a week and the average purse was up around $3,000—about $500 to win. Over the years, Schindler won four American Racing Drivers Club (ARDC) midget championships.

As the midget racing craze died out a few years later Schindler spent more time in the sprint cars, at Indy, and on the AAA championship trail. In 1951 and 1952 Bill Schindler had winnings of $34,959 and posted a win at Springfield, Illinois. Tragically, Schindler died in a sprint car crash at Allentown, Pennsylvania, on September 20, 1952.

There is no doubt that Schindler was a born leader. He was president of the American Racing Drivers Club for six of the eight years that he was a member. It would probably be easier to lead an army than to keep the ARDC running smoothly during those busy years of the midgets. Off the track, he was a family man and a single parent. His son,

Bill Schindler relaxes before a National Championship race at Bay Meadows, California, in the early 1950s (Dennis Arnold photograph).

Bobby, suffered from tuberculosis of the spine and Bill devoted every spare moment to his care and that of his daughter, Doris. It was well hidden from rivals at the time, but Schindler was a talented cook and cake decorator.

Bronco Bill Schindler was one of the most extraordinary men in the annals of auto racing.

Thanks to Doris Schindler of Irving, Texas, for her help with this brief biography of her dad.

The Joe Freeman Collection

One of the better collections of eastern racing photos appearing in this book is the Joe Freeman Collection. Freeman is a Boston vintage sports and race car collector and enthusiast who has also authored articles in *Automobile Quarterly*. The original source of the photos is unknown but Joe Freeman was kind enough to allow them to be copied and shared with others. This collection of around 75 photos came via Rhode Island racing historian Bob Silvia and some of the best are shown here.

Unfortunately, there was almost no identification on the photographs. Bob Silvia was able to identify some of the race tracks, but in general the drivers and car owners are unknown. Photo captions are therefore sparse or simply "unknown." The photos were taken mostly in Massachusetts from the early 1920s to around 1940.

A wrecked Peugeot—probably in New Jersey.

Left: Jimmy Murphy at Readville, Massachusetts, in 1924. Murphy, the 1922 Indy winner, was killed at Syracuse, New York, later that year. At the right is "One Eye" Connally—a famed gate-crasher of the era. *Right:* Probably a Duesenberg. *Below:* A typical fairgrounds track—Flemington, New Jersey.

Opposite top: Unknown. *Opposite middle:* New Market, New Jersey. Note the wooden wheels. *Opposite bottom:* Unknown.

Top: Pete Harris—Essex Special at Dover, New Hampshire. *Bottom:* Harley French. He was killed at Manchester, New Hampshire, in 1926.

Top: This is 1923. Al Trepanier at the wheel of the Jack Foley Fronty. *Middle:* Downtown Readville in 1930. A two-man Stutz Eight. *Bottom:* "One Lap" Dolan.

Top: Barrel racing on the beach, probably Old Orchard Beach, Maine, in about 1930. That is a Duesenberg near the barrel and car #7 is Peterson in a Fronty. *Middle:* Milt Marion at Readville in 1936. *Bottom:* Burt Ross at Readville in 1936.

Opposite top: Jimmy Peterson at Readville in a Model A Duesenberg. He was killed at this track. *Opposite bottom:* A wonderful action shot at the Brockton Fairgrounds in Massachusetts.

Ernie Gessell in action at Readville in 1936. This deadly track was often dusty.

Myke Collins

Myke Collins had a long career as driver and starter on the East Coast. He is best described as "colorful"—not only for his immaculately prepared race cars and his splendid driving uniforms but also for the loud Hawaiian shirts he favored when starting races. Myke Collins stood out in a crowd.

Collins got involved with racing in the early 1930s at New Market Speedway in New Jersey. He wound up with a big car, minus engine, at no cost, and for a grand total of $50 put together a machine that he raced on tracks in the New York City area. Early in his career he realized that showmanship is a big part of the game—his driving uniform consisted of white flannel pants and a black and orange shirt. Ralph DePalma praised Collins on his apparel and told him, "We are actors, and as such, must dress accordingly." Collins never forgot this sage advice although he does remember that "sometimes the race winnings wouldn't pay my cleaning bills!"

For a time Myke Collins drove for Tony Giardina who had an "Easter Egg" McDowell. The car was painted orchid and tea rose with chrome-plated numbers mounted on half-inch spacers. Collins won a feature with this more-than-colorful race car at Crossbay Speedway for a nice payoff of $190.

Collins married in 1935 and gave up the driving end of the sport. For the next two decades he started big car and midget races as well as sports cars and even some boats. A commercial artist by profession, Myke Collins contributed racing cartoons and drawings to *National Auto Racing News* and also wrote articles for this publication.

Neatly dressed Myke Collins is shown at an unidentified eastern track in about 1934. The car is the Tony Giardina "Easter Egg" McDowell (Collins collection).

The First Super Speedway

South Carolina's Darlington is generally considered to be the first of the so-called "Super Speedways" that had become almost commonplace. It turns out that this is not so. The distinction of having the first Super Speedway goes to little old Rhode Island!

The track was built at Narragansett Park in Cranston, a few miles south of Providence. This was the old Rhode Island State Fairgrounds and the same location where the first oval-track race in the United States was held on September 7, 1896. Narragansett Speedway was built in 1915 and was a one-mile banked asphalt oval. Not only were banked tracks (other than the board speedways) almost unheard of in 1915, but paved tracks were equally rare. The paving industry was in its infancy, and special equipment had to be developed to pave the turns which appear to be banked at about twenty degrees.

The first race was held on September 18, 1915. It was under AAA sanction and many of the Indy cars and drivers were on hand. Drivers like Ralph DePalma, Eddie Rickenbacker, Ira Vail, Bob Burman and Willy Haupt raced before a capacity crowd that must have numbered at least 50,000. Eddie Rickenbacker was the winner of that first Super Speedway race.

Top: The field roars into the first turn at Narragansett Speedway on September 18, 1915. The pole driver is unknown but Bob Burman is in #2 and Ira Vail in #4 (Joe Freeman collection—Estey photograph from Bob Silvia). *Bottom:* Action entering the second turn at the end of the backstretch. The backstretch is now Fiat Street in Cranston—and that house is still there! (Joe Freeman collection—Fales photograph from Bob Silvia).

Narragansett Speedway operated from 1915 until 1923—it is believed that all races were big-time events with AAA sanctioning. Details of these races are missing as are the lap times—with that banking, speeds must have been comparable to Indianapolis.

Most of us figure that Rhode Island is too small to have a race track. Local racing historian Bob Silvia will go along with the gag and say that. "The straightaway at Narragansett ran the entire length of the state!" Rhode Island was decades ahead of the rest of the country in race track design. Obviously, we all should have more respect for our smallest state!

The photograph is blurred but the high banking of Narragansett Speedway is evident. One has to wonder just how the primitive grading and paving equipment of the day constructed this track (Joe Freeman collection—Fales Photo from Bob Silvia).

The Bentley

Most likely only one Bentley-powered big car was built. This car, the Lacerox Bentley, raced in the New England states and was driven by Henry Turgeon.

The Bentley was a British car first produced in 1919. The Lacerox big car appears to be constructed from a slightly modified Bentley chassis. It looks like a Model A front axle has been grafted on, but the wheelbase is probably standard Bentley—note that the tail section barely reaches the differential. The radiator shell is Bentley from the mid-1920s. Bentley made a number of different engines so just what

Henry Turgeon in the Lacerox Bentley in about 1938. The unusual car appears heavy and it is doubtful if it was a winner (Bob Silvia collection).

the power plant of the big car was is anybody's guess. Most likely, it was a 270-cubic-inch single-overhead-cam four.

It is not known how the Bentley performed in dirt track races, but one from 1927 to 1930 Bentley won the Le Mans 24-hour race. Bentley showed up at Indy in 1922 and W. Douglas Hawkes finished 13th at a pace some 20 MPH slower than winner Jimmy Murphy.

The *Big*, Big Car

Perhaps the biggest big car ever to compete in a dirt track race was the machine entered by Doc Morris in a 1934 event at Readville, Massachusetts.

Doc Morris had wrecked his big car and there wasn't time to fix it for the Readville race. Morris heard about a 1932 Auburn four-door Sedan that had burned and managed to locate owner Gordon Berry. After a bit of haggling Berry agreed to let Morris cut the sedan body off the chassis and build something that resembled a race car. The deal was that Morris would pay the entry fee, and all winnings would be split 50-50. The Auburn had a two speed rear end and a 276-cubic-inch straight-eight engine that put out something like 100 horsepower—it was also about two blocks long and must have weighed two tons. From the junk yard came some scrap metal that Morris fashioned into a pointed race car tail. He was ready to go at Readville on July 4, 1934.

Doc Morris timed in at 55.0 seconds on the one-mile oval and was tied for second-quickest time. By lap 14 in the 25-mile main event Morris took his bulky machine to the front of an eight-car field. Lap 19 brought near disaster as a right rear tire blew out and Doc spun out in a huge cloud of dust. Undaunted, he kept right on going even though, after a few laps, the tire flew off and Morris was left with only the wheel rim. Morris finished the race in second place—possibly the best ever performance by an Auburn "big car." The payoff was $40, but when Morris presented Gordon Berry with his $20 share he was informed that he owed two dollars for the blown tire. Berry got the two bucks.

9

East

Pennsylvania, New Jersey, Maryland, Delaware, West Virginia, Virginia

This is a densely populated area and, as one would expect, a lot of racing went on during the 1920s and 1930s.

In Pennsylvania racing got under way on May 30, 1904, at Point Breeze, a one-mile horse track near Philadelphia. There were road races at Fairmount Park in that same city that reportedly attracted 400,000 fans in 1908. Later on Philadelphia had racing at the Belmont and Byberry tracks. Pittsburgh racing began in 1907 at Brunots Island—a horse track on an Ohio River island. With the exception of one race at an unnamed track there was probably no dirt track racing in the Pittsburgh area until New Kensington opened in 1931. In 1919 racing started at the Allentown Fairgrounds and continued for well over 50 years. The Altoona Fairgrounds held intermittent racing from 1913 to 1920—this was a different site from the Altoona board track which had a dirt oval after the board era. In DuBois racing went on from 1916 to 1941 at the Gateway Fairgrounds. At Hatfield the half-mile dirt oval saw action from 1922 until 1951. Jennerstown Speedway ran from 1927 until after World War II. Reading had some great racing started in 1924 and it continued until 1979. Other Pennsylvania towns that hosted races included Clarion, Clearfield, Bird-In-Hand, Indiana, Shickshinny, and Kutztown. And then there was Langhorne! This circular one-mile speedway was located just northeast of Philadelphia. Langhorne had its ups and downs, scared a lot of drivers, and had no equal in the world. A book could, and should, be written about this place.

New Jersey racing started in Trenton at the Inter-State Fairgrounds on September 24, 1900, and racing on this half-mile oval continued until 1945. Several other New Jersey cities had pre–World War I racing including Guttenburg, Flemington, the Monmouth Fairgrounds near Oceanport, and—surprisingly—Ho-Ho-Kus. This track ran some famous 1930s races and was probably responsible for getting Chris Economaki hooked on racing. Flemington had racing from 1910 to 1966. New

Top: Just who the lady is or where the photograph was taken is unknown, but this car was driven in the 1919 Indy race by Ora Haibe. The factory Hudson qualified at 92.80 MPH and finished the 500 mile race in 14th position (Harold Osmer collection). *Bottom:* Dirt track action someplace in the Baltimore area in about 1920. Obviously a horse-racing facility but definitely not the famed Pimlico track (Don Moore collection).

Top: Dusty action at an unknown track. The date is around 1920. *Bottom:* Early action shots like this are rare. This appears to be a race at a rather run-down horse racing facility. Sadly, no identification (Both photographs—Don Moore collection).

The lineup at Luna Park in Johnstown, Pennsylvania, in August of 1921. This track was built for the horses in 1910 and hosted a few auto races over the years. This is an event for local cars (Billy Horner collection).

Market Speedway ran from 1928 until 1934 and Mt. Holly had intermittent racing in the 1920s and 1930s. Union Speedway in Union saw racing from 1936 to 1940. Woodbridge had a half-mile dirt oval that ran before the better-known board track was built in 1928 and after the demise of the wood track in 1932. Other New Jersey race locations included Troy Hills, Freehold and Camden.

Maryland's first racing was at Electric Park in Baltimore on November 22, 1900. A few years later there was auto racing at the now-famous Pimlico horse track in Baltimore. A couple of races were held in 1908, and perhaps other races in the 1930s, but this later racing could not be verified. A track adjacent to Pimlico, called The Gentlemen's Driving Park, might have held races in about 1916, but most likely was just an oval where "gentlemen" could test their stock cars. Frederick had a half-mile track at the fairgrounds where racing started sometime in the 1910s and continued until 1977. Hagerstown had a track that operated in the 1920s. The 1930s saw racing at places like Bel Aire, Cambridge, Brooklyn, and Salisbury. There was a half-mile track at Laureldale that had racing in about 1934 or 1935 but the town has been forgotten—it is not on modern maps.

The District of Columbia doesn't rate mention in the heading of this chapter, but it did have some big car racing. There was a Benning Speedway that held races on a half-mile track on September 6, 1915, June 5, 1937, and maybe a few other races in 1937. One can only wonder where this track was located in the densely populated city of Washington, D.C.

In Delaware there was no known racing until 1921. This was at the Kent-Sussex County Fairgrounds in Harrington. This site became the Delaware State Fairgrounds in 1962 and races are still held there. Other sites where there was racing in

Top: This is Somerset, Pennsylvania, in the early 1920s. Not much is known about the photograph other than "Gerster," of Somerset is in #5 trailing the field (Billy Horner collection). *Middle:* Art Stewart drove this Fronty Ford in New Jersey races in 1929 (Don Radbruch collection). *Bottom:* This photograph is a total mystery. It is obviously a AAA race and probably in Pennsylvania—but where and when? (Jim Way collection).

Top: This is one of an unknown number of Hisso-powered cars built by the Ambler brothers. Let's hope that is an oil tank and not the fuel tank in front of the radiator. *Middle:* Len Perry drove this nice-looking Green Special at Troy Hills, New Jersey in about 1933 (Top and middle photographs—Harold Osmer collection). *Bottom:* Wild Bill Cassidy takes a wild spill at the Arden Downs track, Washington, Pennsylvania. Cassidy survived this July 12, 1936, crash but was seriously injured (Magazine photograph from the John Way collection).

the 1930s are Augustine Beach Speedway in Fort Penn, the Eslmere Fairgrounds, New Castle, Milford, and Volunteer Speedway at Rehobeth Beach. These are the only recorded race locations in Delaware.

West Virginia racing may have started in the 1910s at Moundsville in the northern part of the state. There was a motorcycle race there in 1915 and perhaps the autos ran at about the same time. Clarksburg had racing from 1921 until 1940. At Elkins race cars ran in the 1920s and 1930s. Slim Rutherford is recorded as a consistent winner at Parkersburg in 1924 and racing continued there until the 1930s. There was racing at Pennsboro in the 1920s, and this has continued intermittently to the present. Other West Virginia race tracks include Wheeling Downs, Romney, and Spencer.

It was in 1917 that racing started in Virginia. This was on a one-mile track at the Virginia State

Right: Ken Fowler at an eastern track in about 1936. Fowler was involved in a spectacular midget crash at the opening of Nutley Stadium in 1938 when he crashed into the grandstands injuring 13 people. He later became a top USAC official. *Bottom:* Gus Zarka was one of the better East Coast drivers. Zarka drove in the 1936–37 Vanderbilt Cup Races on Long Island in cars owned by the Ambler brothers—machines probably powered by Hissos (Both photographs—Jim Way collection).

Fairgrounds in Richmond. Races were held on this oval until about 1919, and later a half-mile oval was constructed at the same site that saw action from 1929 to 1947. Norfolk had three 1920s and '30s tracks. Two of these were Dixie Speedway and the Norfolk Fairgrounds—clever scheduling resulted in both tracks running on May 30, 1924. The third speedway was Princess Anne that operated in the 1930s. The Roanoke Fairgrounds apparently had only one race—a AAA event in about 1934. Other Virginia tracks were located at Staunton, Suffolk, and Winchester.

Top: The pits at Ho-Ho-Kus, New Jersey, in about 1935. The track drew good fields of cars and good crowds from nearby New York City (Don Radbruch collection). *Middle:* Although better-known for his midget exploits, Cowboy O'Rourke also took a few big car rides. Note the strange engine setup on this car with the carburetors below the exhaust headers—what on earth is it? (Jim Way collection). *Bottom:* Ernie Gessell was another well-known midget pilot who drove the big cars. Here he is in the Williams McDowell at an unknown track (Marty Brightman collection).

Top: Herman Schurch in about 1930. Schurch starred at Langhorne and other eastern tracks before heading for Legion Ascot in 1931. He died in a practice crash at that deadly place a few weeks after his arrival (Jim Way collection). *Middle:* When the "champ cars" ran at Langhorne in 1934 it was the two man cars. This is Joe Russo in the Forman Axle car that Lou Moore drove to a third place finish at Indy in 1934. Russo was killed at Langhorne—possibly on this day. *Bottom:* Langhorne in 1934. Fred Frame owned this Duesenberg and probably drove it on this day. Rex Mays had driven the car at Indy—his first appearance in the 500 (Lower photographs—Harold Osmer collection).

Top: Floyd Roberts at Langhorne in 1938. This is the same car he drove to victory at Indy earlier that year. *Middle:* Floyd Jarvie at Langhorne in about 1940. This is the Derrimann car that Billy Winn died in at Springfield, Illinois, in 1938. *Bottom:* Mauri Rose is almost lost in the cockpit of the Burd Piston Ring Special at Langhorne. Rose co-drove this car (with Floyd Davis) to victory in the 1941 Indy 500 (All photographs—Jim Way collection).

Top: Tony Willman was one of the greatest drivers of the late 1930s and early 1940s. He had four Indy starts, won 97 midget features, and had 31 big car victories. He's shown here at Indianapolis in 1941. Willman died in a crash at Thompson Speedway on October 12, 1941 (Osmer collection). *Middle:* Rex Records in 1939. Records competed mostly in the midgets and was still winning races as late as 1948. *Bottom:* A candid shot of the great Rex Mays. Probably 1939 and at Langhorne (Lower photographs—Jim Way collection).

Top: Ted Horn grabs the lead at Reading, Pennsylvania. The year is about 1939, the starter is Don Gernere, and it is not known who is driving #28. Reading drew huge crowds for auto races. *Bottom:* Walt Ader talks things over with a well dressed group before a race at Reading, Pennsylvania, in 1939. Ader tried to qualify at Indy from 1948 to 1950 but failed to make the show (Both photographs—Jim Way collection).

Top: Bob Sall in the beautiful Peters Miller in about 1940. The photograph appears to have been taken at "Gasoline Alley" in Paterson, New Jersey (Joe Gemsa collection). *Middle:* Three legends of the sport warm up at Union, New Jersey, in about 1936. Left to right are Bob Sall, Doc MacKenzie and Floyd Davis. Union Speedway operated from 1936 to 1940 (Don Radbruch collection). *Bottom:* Warmups at Trenton in 1939. That's Joie Chitwood in the Hank O'Day Offy in the foreground. Racing at the New Jersey Fairgrounds half-miler went on from 1900 to 1941. A one-mile track, later paved, was built at the same site after World War II (Herbert Anderson collection from Bill Hill).

Chris

He is the only man active in prewar racing who is still on the job today. He is a man who has served as mechanic for one of racing's greats. He even had a brief stint at driving, but his huge contribution to racing has been from behind a typewriter or a microphone. Millions of people have read his stories, seen him at racetracks all over the world and enjoyed his comments on TV. It is hard to call one man "Mr. Auto Racing" but maybe this guy is just that—he is Chris Economaki.

Chris Economaki has been around auto racing for nearly 70 years. It all began in the small town of Ridgewood, New Jersey, when the 11-year-old Chris discovered what was making all that racket on Saturday afternoons. It was the roar of racing engines at Ho-Ho-Kus Speedway a couple of miles away. Chris was lucky in that his barber was the father of racer Bob Sall. Before long Mr. Sall was taking Chris along to races, not only at Ho-Ho-Kus, but at tracks like Woodbridge, Allentown, Reading and Langhorne.

By 1934 Chris and a friend had started a small racing photo business. They had ads in the newly born *National Auto Racing News* that was printed in Ridgewood. The paper came out on Wednesday nights and the two youngsters would be on hand to get a copy of the paper and see their ads. Because Chris went to so many races the editor of the paper asked him to write an occasional story. His first byline came from a Flemington Fairgrounds race late in 1935. Payment? No way! This was the first of hundreds or maybe thousands of "freebies" that Chris Economaki wrote for *NARN*. Things worked out OK though as this newspaper is now *National Speed Sport News*, the nation's leading racing publication. Chris actually went to work for the newspaper with a paycheck in the late 1940s and took over as editor and publisher in 1950. He later became part owner of the publication, and today enjoys the title of Editor and Publisher Emeritus. He still writes a popular weekly column that is the backbone of the newspaper.

Chris Economaki is shown with A.J. Foyt some years ago. The two could be discussing something important regarding racing, but Chris recalls, "We were comparing broken arms." (Chris Economaki collection).

Economaki's involvement with the "get dirty" end of racing was in the late 1930s when he acted as mechanic on Duane Carter's Elto engined midget. This would have to be what today is a "Crew Chief," for Chris received the lofty salary of

$15 a week—even though he was lucky to get paid one week out of four. The money didn't matter—it was racing, and heaven.

Chris' driving career was brief and scary. He describes this 1939 adventure in an article by Bob Cutter in the 1984 special 50th Anniversary Issue of *National Speed Sport News*.

"I went to Ashley, Pennsylvania, with Dave Randolph and had my chance in a cycle midget which they called "shakers" in those days. I found out why. The car shook so much I could hardly see in my borrowed crash helmet which was substantially too large. It was traumatic going around that fifth-mile. The purse that night—for everybody—was $340. I didn't see any of it. I did worse than poorly. Finish? I felt lucky to be alive after the race."

In retrospect, millions of us are lucky that Chris Economaki was something less than a natural behind the wheel of a race car. Through the media, he's shared his knowledge and enthusiasm for racing with all of us. Thanks, Chris!

Central Pennsy

One of the strongest groups in eastern racing in the mid-1930s was the Central Pennsy Racing Association. Headquartered at Central Speedway in Bird-In-Hand, Pennsylvania, this group attracted some of the best drivers in the East as well as developing its own stars.

Central Pennsy's drivers raced at the Pennsylvania towns of Bird-In Hand, Lebanon, Lehighton, Landisville, Hughesville, Clearfield and Bedford. The purses were not large, usually less than $300, but the group had full fields at most of their races. All of the cars appeared to be home built and most were primitive, crude and less than beautiful. Most of the drivers achieved only local recognition—men like Dutch Culp, Al Gasta, Johnny Zohmer, Paul Young, Dutch Scollenberger, Ammon Kelchner, and Dave Wilt. A few drivers, like Mark Light, Otis Stine, and Ted Nyquist became some of the best drivers

Recognize this guy? A young Tommy Hinnershitz—'The Flying Farmer"—at Central Speedway at Bird-In-Hand on August 21, 1935. Hinnershitz drove the Kaufman Cragar to a heat-race win and a second in the feature. The payoff was probably $44. Tommy later drove at Indianapolis.

Top: Paul Young in 1936. Young had already won the Central Pennsy championship in 1938 when he was killed at Lebanon. *Middle left:* Tex Arnz is shown with car owner Ebby Ebersole in 1936. Arnz was a better-than-average driver who later won some races in John Gerber's car. *Middle right:* Ammon Kelchner was one of the stars of the Central Pennsy Racing Association. He was killed in a 1940 crash at Altoona, Pennsylvania. *Bottom:* Mark Light at Central Speedway in 1935. Light won the 1936 Central Pennsy title and was well on his way to repeating in 1937 when he was injured at Lebanon. Light later had a long career as a promoter. (All photographs—Jim Way collection).

Top: John Favinger drove this scary-looking creation in Central Pennsy races in 1934. *Middle left:* Al Gasta never won a feature race but he was always there trying. He was fatally injured at Lebanon on November 1, 1936. *Middle right:* Dave Wilt at Bird-In-Hand in 1935. His #2 has an Ambler engine, and yes, that is stove pipe serving as an exhaust pipe. *Bottom:* The field gets going at Lebanon in 1937. Mark Light is on the pole with Ted Nyquist on the outside. (All photographs—Jim Way collection).

Top left: Art Heber in his SO McDowell in about 1936. Some of the Central Pennsy cars had good engines despite their primitive appearance. *Top right:* Johnny Zohmer—real name, Border McKean. He won some Central Pennsy races before dying in a 1936 crash at Lebanon. *Middle:* An unknown driver in the Kauffman SO Hal in about 1936. Despite its ungainly appearance it is believed that this is the same car that finished in paying positions in 48 of 61 races in 1937. Mark Light and Paul Young were the drivers. *Bottom:* The remains of the Kaufmann Hal engine after it blew up in 1938. The ensuing fire resulted in fatal burns to driver Paul Young.

Top: O.R. Peterson drove this Whippet-powered machine in Central Pennsy races. While not overly popular, the Whippet did make a competitive racing engine, and speed equipment was available. *Middle:* Ford V-8 engines were rare in mid–1930s race cars but this Central Pennsy machine had one. Paul Young is the driver. *Bottom:* This McDowell was thoroughly bent in a 1935 crash at Central Speedway in Bird-In-Hand (All photographs—Jim Way collection).

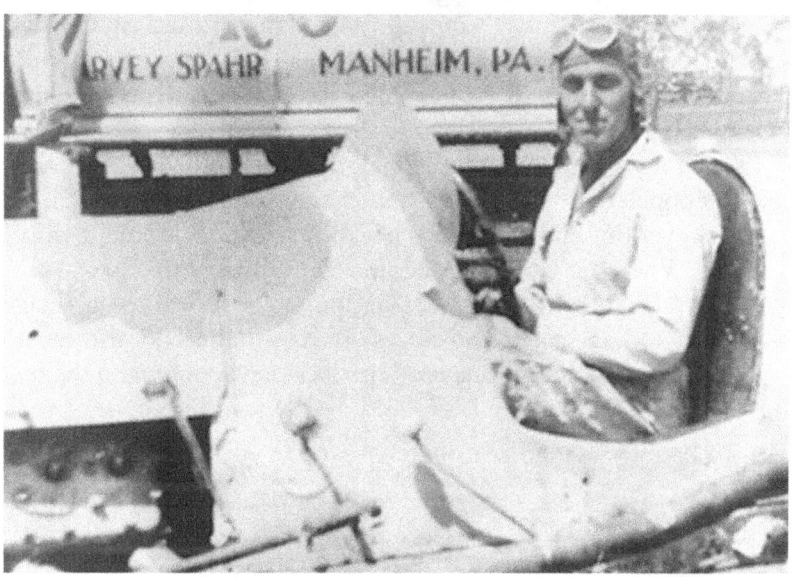

in the East. A young fellow named Tommy Hinnershitz also raced with the Central Pennsy group.

Sadly, at least a half dozen Central Pennsy drivers lost their lives in a few short years.

"By J. Earl Way"

Remember that byline? If you are a long time reader of racing publications that name may ring a bell. J. Earl Way covered both big car and midget racing in the Pennsylvania area for many years.

His interest in racing was almost accidental. J. Earl Way was a barber in the small central Pennsylvania town of Salunga, and in 1932 was also the coach of the local semi-professional football team. As an added attraction the football team began holding jalopy races at half time. The races, on a rough oval around the gridiron, soon proved more popular than the football games: so popular that football was soon forgotten in Salunga and jalopy racing took over. The ticket seller cashed in on this popularity by (allegedly) pocketing some of the cash. J. Earl Way was asked to take over this chore and thus began years of involvement with Pennsylvania racing.

When big car racing became prevalent in the area, Way helped organize the Central Pennsy Racing Association. Way served as secretary for the association and acted as scorer and occasional announcer at the races. Most importantly, Way wrote about the races for both local newspapers and the then-emerging *National Auto Racing News*. There is no doubt that his efforts helped make the Central Pennsy Racing Association a remarkably strong group.

In the late 1930s Way kept busy handling the publicity for promoters like Ralph Hankinson at Reading and Langhorne. He helped promote races at Williams Grove and the very successful midget racing at Hershey, Pennsylvania. Remarkably, J. Earl Way accomplished this while operating his Salunga barbershop from 9 A.M. to 9 P.M. five days a week—

J. Earl Way is shown at Lebanon, Pennsylvania in 1938. He's flanked by two of racing's greats—Joie Chitwood on the left and Ted Horn on the right. In his lifetime Way was acquainted with many of the legends of racing (Jim Way collection).

including Saturdays. His son, Jim, remembers long all-night drives to get to the race tracks by Sunday morning.

J. Earl Way continued to be active in racing through the 1950s. He gave a lot to Pennsylvania auto racing.

The Match Races at Johnstown

It is probable that Johnstown's primary claim to fame is being washed away in a flood, but the western Pennsylvania city did host some auto races. One event was held on September 6, 1919, and featured Gaston Chevrolet and Omar Toft in a series of match races.

Both drivers had competed in a board track race at Uniontown, Pennsylvania, a few days earlier—Chevrolet won the 225-mile event in his Frontenac and Toft was credited with 12th place after experiencing engine trouble with his Miller. Gaston Chevrolet was a legitimate racing star, but Toft, billed as the "undefeated Pacific Coast Dirt Track Champion," was sometimes involved in shady deals. If one believes the pre-race publicity both Toft and Chevrolet posted $2,500 side bets before the races.

According to the *Johnstown Tribune*, the series of six-to-ten-lap match races at the Luna Park half-mile oval "attracted a crowd of 4500 enthusiastic auto race fans." Chevrolet won the first race but Toft came back to capture the next two events in a row. Chevrolet won the next, setting up a winner take all final. Why are you not surprised? Toft had engine problems and Gaston Chevrolet easily won the final, and took home the $5,000.

According to the *Tribune* Chevrolet "was forced to smash all track records to defeat his opponent—at one point traveling a mile in one minute flat." This was a full ten seconds under the track record—not bad for a board-track Indy car. It is a little bit surprising, but the obviously hippodromed events were with the AAA's blessing if not an outright sanction. One has to wonder if other Uniontown racers competed in similar events at other Pennsylvania towns on the same weekend. Johnstown had hosted a AAA race in 1914 and local events were held at the Luna Park track in the early 1920s.

(Thanks to Billy Horner of Johnstown for the above information.)

The Mysterious Mr. Chamberlain

Ted Chamberlain's name appears in racing history over a span of twenty years. He shows up at a major race and then disappears for a couple of years or a decade. The records of most drivers can be traced more or less continuously—not so for Ted Chamberlain.

He first emerges at Indianapolis in 1930 as a relief driver for Joe Huff in the

Ted Chamberlain did get his picture taken at Lebanon in 1936. This is the only known photograph of the nebulous Mr. Chamberlain (Jim Way collection).

Gauss Front Drive Miller Eight. In 1931 he was back at Indy as the driver of the Searles Miller and qualified as first alternate for the race. Five years pass by and Theodore Chamberlain, driving the Wingarter Duesenberg, takes part in the Vanderbilt Cup race on Long Island.

Chamberlain next shows up in, of all places, the NASCAR stockers. In early 1952 he drove at Macon, Georgia, and at Langhorne. His best finish was at Langhorne where he drove a '50 Plymouth to a 14th place finish for a payoff of $25.

In 1936 Chamberlain stopped at Salunga, Pennsylvania, for a haircut at J. Earl Way's barbershop. Chamberlain noticed the racing photos on the wall, mentioned that he'd driven at Indy, and soon he and Way were deeply involved in racing talk. The upshot of this was that Chamberlain was invited to a Central Pennsy Racing Association event at Lebanon the following day. He managed to talk his way into a hot laps ride in Herm Kaufman's Cragar, and reportedly emerged a bit shaken by the speed of the home-built car. The next day Chamberlain resumed his journey, and so far as anybody knows, he never returned to central Pennsylvania. In later years J. Earl Way tried to trace Chamberlain but came up empty.

There has to be a beginning to Ted Chamberlain's racing career—something before Indy in 1930. There has to be more to the middle of his career and maybe something after 1952. Does anybody know?

Troy Hills

Troy Hills Speedway in northeastern New Jersey was typical of independent tracks that operated in the early 1930s. Located near the village of Parsippany, the one-third-mile oval ran with moderate success from around 1931 to 1934. Thanks to Crocky Wright of Speedway, Indiana, complete data on the 1933 season at Troy Hills is available.

The track ran a total of 31 events in 1933 despite being plagued by occasional car shortages and having races sanctioned by three different organizations. The first sanctioning body was the National Auto Racing Association (NARA). This group was soon short of cars and aligned itself with another independent group, the Auto Racing Association (ARA). This was nice, but at the next race none of the ARA drivers showed up—it seems a conflicting race had been scheduled. Only a few NARA cars were on hand and they ran a couple of exhibition heat events—stock car roadsters completed the remainder of the program. (This is the first recorded roadster racing in New Jersey.) On June 21, the Garden State Racing Association (GSRA) took over the track and the remainder of the season was apparently hassle-free, with ARA support and adequate fields of cars.

Troy Hills was one of the first eastern tracks to install lights and run the full-sized race cars at night. To Gus Ianacone went the honor of winning the first night race on May 26, 1933. The big winners at Troy Hills during the 1933 season were Harry Angeloni and Bob Becktloff, with main event wins also going to Frankie Bailey, Johnny Ulesky, Bill Holmes, Frank Curtis and Jack Moon. No track champion was crowned, but the race results show it would have been Angeloni or Becktloff.

Troy Hills ran for at least three years without a driver fatality—a rarity in those days. Its relatively short length and the fact that it was "paved" with a mixture of something called "mine dust" and road oil probably contributed to the excellent safety record. The track apparently closed after the 1934 season and, in Crocky Wright's words, "went to the dogs," and became a dog-racing facility. This was unsuccessful and houses were soon built on the site of Troy Hills Speedway.

Williams Grove

Williams Grove Speedway at Mechanicsburg, Pennsylvania, has long been one of the finest race tracks in the East. From the beginning on May 31, 1939, Williams Grove attracted the best cars and drivers in the nation—and it still does.

The following photos are just a sample of the great drivers who competed at Williams Grove in the years before World War II.

A group photograph at Williams Grove in 1939. Left to right are Spider Webb, Duke Nalon, Len Duncan, Jimmy Knight, Mr. Shelley, Ted Horn, Walt Brown, Russ Snowberger, Joie Chitwood, and promoter Roy Richwine. (Jim Way collection).

Top: Rex Records. *Middle:* Russ Snowberger. *Bottom:* Mike Little (All photographs—Jim Way collection).

Top: Len Duncan. *Middle:* Bill Holland. *Bottom:* Hank Rogers (All photographs—Jim Way collection).

Top: Vic Nauman *Bottom:* Ammon Kelchner (Both photographs—Jim Way collection).

10

South

*Kentucky, Tennessee, Arkansas,
Alabama, Mississippi, Louisiana*

As in some other areas, racing in this section of the United States is very poorly documented. Major racing groups, like the IMCA and AAA, made occasional visits into this area and some record of this exists. There had to have been local groups in the South—perhaps half a dozen of them—but the details are seemingly long gone.

Kentucky first saw racing on May 23, 1906, when a reported 36,000 fans turned out at Lexington to see a show promoted by Bill Pickens and Barney Oldfield. Five years later Oldfield won a race at Covington and is said to have driven the same Marmon that Ray Harroun used to win the first Indy 500 a couple of weeks later. Louisville had racing on a mile horse track from about 1909 until 1929 and at the Kentucky State Fairgrounds from 1918 to 1932, with a few races after that year. The Kentucky Motor Speedway in Louisville was a half-mile oval that ran from 1926 to 1932. Fulton, Lebanon, Hartford and Ashland all had some racing in the 1930s. Most of the towns mentioned above are in areas adjacent to Kentucky's northern neighbors of Illinois, Indiana and Ohio so odds are many of the racers were from these states.

In Tennessee there was racing at Nashville as early as 1907 and at Memphis and Chattanooga in 1914 and 1917. Nashville began having annual races as part of the Tennessee State Fair in 1915. In the first races four drivers and one spectator were fatally injured. Racing continued at Nashville until 1941 and resumed after World War II. The racing at Chattanooga was probably also part of an annual fair and this continued to 1936. It was much the same thing at Memphis, where there was fairgrounds racing until 1941. The 1920s and '30s races at Nashville, Chattanooga and Memphis were no doubt under the sanction of the AAA or the IMCA. In the late 1930s and early '40s, racing at Johnson City, Murfreesboro, and two other Chattanooga tracks, Camp Foster and Warner Park, was probably with local cars.

The first known racing in Arkansas was on October 10, 1918, at Jonesboro. This

Top: Ben Gotoff at the 1922 Louisiana State Fair in Shreveport. There is some evidence that this is a Miller and—with those front wheel brakes—it could be an Indy or board track car but this could not be confirmed (Tom Saal collection). *Bottom:* This is a race for black drivers. The location is unknown but it is probably someplace in the South (Ray Valasek collection).

was probably an IMCA event or some other touring group. There was also racing in this city in the 1930s. At Little Rock racing began at the Arkansas State Fairgrounds in 1925 and continued until about 1937. Fayetteville had racing in 1932, and Blytheville from 1938 until 1941. Some of this racing might have been IMCA, or even AAA, but it is also possible that there was some sort of Arkansas racing group that was active in the 1930s.

Birmingham had the first racing in Alabama on a one-mile track at the state fairgrounds. Racing continued on this oval until 1917. Later on, a half-mile track was built at the fairgrounds and this saw racing action starting in 1933, with AAA stars at some of the events. Andalusia had races in 1921 and 1922 at the Covington

County Fairgrounds. At Dothan there was 1920s racing and Opelika also had a track that operated around the same time. On the Gulf coast Mobile had racing from around 1921 to 1935. In Huntsville there was racing during the 1920s at the Madison County Fairgrounds. Both the IMCA and AAA ran in Alabama but other races were by an independent group—possibly from Florida.

The known racing in Mississippi is confined to four tracks. The first racing was in 1903 at the Mississippi State Fairgrunds in Jackson and this continued until 1937. In Meridian racing got underway in 1917 at the Mississippi-Alabama State Fairgrounds and continued until 1937. Tupelo also had a Mississippi-Alabama State Fairgrounds and held races in 1927 and in the 1930s. Laurel had a half-miler that ran from about 1927 to 1941. Some of the above tracks held races after World War II, but odds are these were stock car events.

October 22, 1941, and the IMCA is at the Louisiana State Fair. Three of the IMCA's best drivers pose for the cameraman. Left to right are Gus Schrader, Ben Shaw and Jimmy Wilburn. Gus Schrader was fatally injured on this day (Bob Hagen collection).

Louisiana had racing on but a few tracks. At Shreveport racing started on November 10, 1910, and Barney Oldfield won that race. This Louisiana State Fairgrounds track was a one-mile oval and remained in use until 1936. A half-mile track was built in 1931 and this saw action until 1941 and then again after the war. The Mardi Gras track in New Orleans held races from 1909 until 1918 and then a race in May of 1921. At Plaucheville a dirt oval operated, probably briefly, in about 1921. In 1941 there were races at Baton Rouge and Covington, but at that late date these were probably for stock cars.

Fred Horey

Fred Horey was one of the best drivers in the 1910s and 1920s. Like so many fine drivers of the era his story could have been lost to racing history. Fortunately it was not thanks to an extensive scrapbook kept primarily by Fred's wife Hazel. Clippings from newspaper all over the United States and Canada plus hundreds of photographs tell the story of Fred Horey's career and, as a bonus, a bit about the drivers Fred raced against.

Fred Horey first appears at the board track in Oakland, California, in 1911. It is unclear if he actually raced on this half-mile high-banked circle, but there is a photo of him in one of the racing cars. Later that same year Fred was in the training camp of the Case racing team in Savannah, Georgia. In 1913 he was at Indianapolis as riding mechanic for Joe Nikrant. In 1915 the International Motor Contest Association (IMCA) was formed and Fred Horey was one of the group's first star

drivers. For the next dozen years Horey crisscrossed the United States and Canada with J. Alex Sloan's touring IMCA drivers. There were hundreds of races in big cities and small towns. It was "show biz" and Horey and the other drivers routinely set "world records." Somewhat surprisingly the IMCA did not bother to crown a champion until 1925 when Fred Horey became the first champion—a feat he repeated in 1926.

Fred Horey spent almost all of his career in the IMCA. To be sure, some of the races were

Left: Fred Horey in about 1920. That backwards cap was his trademark "crash helmet" for many years. *Bottom:* This is probably Columbus, Ohio, in about 1920. Horey's car is in the middle of the pack.

hippodromes with planned results, but Horey was making a comfortable living and saw no need to bolt to the AAA or worry about Indianapolis. There were also family ties as his sister was married to J. Alex Sloan. Fred Horey was a great race driver—we'll never know just how good he was.

A special thank you to Fred Horey's daughter, Christine Horey Logan, for sharing the material in this wonderful scrapbook. And a thank you to Christine's friend, Grace Jones, for spending countless hours making remarkably clear copies of the clippings and photographs.

Top: Fred Horey takes the checkered flag at an unknown track. *Bottom:* Another unknown track and another close win for Fred Horey in #4.

Top: Fred Horey at Waco, Texas, in October of 1922. Is the car a Fiat? *Left:* Fred Horey has won a beautiful silver trophy at an unknown track. (Both photographs—Christine Horey Logan collection from Grace Jones.)

Shreveport, October 22, 1941

In the past ten or so years many historians have written thousands of words about Gus Schrader's fatal accident at Shreveport, Louisiana, on October 22, 1941. Despite as much research as can be done many years after the fact, the cause of the crash remains a mystery.

This is one version of the crash and may or may not be accurate: Schrader and Jimmy Wilburn were racing wheel to wheel, but their cars almost certainly did not touch. Maybe some sort of mechanical defect caused Schrader's car to suddenly flip upside down. Maybe the car got too much "side bite?"

The remains of Gus Schrader's car after his fatal wreck on October 22, 1941 (Roy Eaton collection).

Schrader died when he was thrown from the car and his helmet came off upon impact with the ground. Gus Schrader never used a seat belt.

As indicated by the photo below, Schrader's 318 Offy Riverside Tire Special was only slightly damaged in the crash. Almost certainly Gus Schrader would have been OK had he been using a seat belt and stayed with the car.

To the mystery and controversy surrounding Gus Schrader's tragic death can be added, "What if?"

11

Southeast
North Carolina, South Carolina, Georgia, Florida

There was a fair amount of racing in these four states, but unfortunately most of the details are missing. The AAA and the IMCA made occasional forays into this area and some of this racing can be documented. There is a bit of information available on the smaller groups that ran in Florida but data on the activities of local racers in the other states is seemingly gone forever.

North Carolina had no known racing until about 1921 when races were held at the Kinston Fairgrounds—possibly only one race was held there. Concord had racing on a half-mile horse track at the Cabarrus District Fairgrounds from 1926 until 1934. In Charlotte dirt track racing got underway in 1926 and continued until 1960 at the Southern States Fairgrounds—the AAA visited this facility in the 1930s and 1940s. Other major cities that had racing were Greensboro, starting in 1926, Raleigh, Rocky Mount and Wilmington. Some of these cities might have been stops on early fall AAA tours. Most of the cities mentioned above are within reasonable trav-

The field lines up for the cameraman at Daytona Beach in 1927. The races were around barrels placed on the beach—probably a half-mile or a mile apart. Due to the difficulty of collecting admission fees the purse was no doubt very low (Glenn McGlonie collection).

eling distance of each other so it seems likely that there was a North Carolina group that raced regularly at these locations.

In South Carolina, there was pre–World War II racing at only four known locations. One of these was Bennettsville, a small town in the northeastern part of the state, where races were held on unknown dates in the 1930s. The larger towns of Columbia and Orangeburg had racing starting in 1932, but by the late 1930s the stock cars had probably taken over. Most of the South Carolina racing was at Spartanburg. Racing began here in 1928 at the Spartanburg Fairgrounds with a AAA event won by Bob Robinson over a field that included Billy Winn and Bob Sall. Races were held here annually as part of the county fair from 1933 to 1938, with AAA sanction except for 1937. (The Spartanburg races from 1937 on were at a different track located at the Piedmont Interstate Fairgrounds.) Notable in 1936 was the entry of Bill France in a Hal big car. In 1939 the stock cars raced during the fair, and it appears the big cars were finished in Spartanburg.

Georgia had racing as early as 1908 on road courses in Savannah. There was also a two-mile dirt oval called the Atlanta Motordrome near the site of the present-day Atlanta International Airport—Ray Harroun won a race there in 1910. Racing continued in Atlanta at the Atlanta Speedway, which had several names, but probably ran races only in 1920–21 and 1929–30. This track, then called Hamilton Speedway, reportedly had a "world's record" of 23.3 seconds on a 35-degree banked dirt track in 1939. Lakewood Speedway in Atlanta opened in 1915 but ran only motorcycles until 1917, when Barney Oldfield and Ralph DePalma won auto races. Over the years Lakewood ran mostly AAA races and is probably best remembered as the scene of some serious crashes. Savannah had racing on a half-mile oval on an apparently

Top: The only thing known about this photograph is that is was taken in Macon, Georgia, in about 1930. This would have to be the one-mile Central City Park Speedway at the Georgia State Fairgrounds. This track operated from the 1920s until 1938 (Joe Cawley collection). *Bottom:* Ray Gast is shown with his race car in about 1930. Gast competed at the Daytona Beach Speedway (not a track—just barrels place on the beach) and on other Florida tracks. Engine type is unknown but the car looks too big for a Model T or A-B (Bob Gast collection).

Top: It is February 1931 at the DeLand Fairgrounds. Ray Gast battles for the lead in the center of the track. The car on the outside, near the rail, may be Hick Jenkins' Essex Four. *Left:* The wide Florida beaches must have provided great places to test race cars. Here the Ray Gast machine is shown on the beach. That's probably Ray's dad in the cockpit and the lady is Mrs. Ray Gast (Both photographs—Bob Gast collection).

intermittent basis from 1924 to 1939. Macon had a one-mile dirt track that ran from the 1920s to 1938, and in Albany there was a half-miler that started operations in the 1920s.

Florida racing began on the beaches in about 1904. Ormond Beach (an extension of Daytona Beach) had not only speed trials but also races around barrels placed six to seven miles apart. There was also early beach racing at Jacksonville and probably at other unrecorded locations. Racing around barrels on Florida's beaches continued throughout the 1920s and 1930s. Much of the activity was at Daytona Beach, which had what sounds like a big-time event in 1922. This race was hyped by none other than Barney Oldfield, and if the pre-race publicity can be believed, Barney's famed "Blitzen Benz" was entered and driven by Jimmy Costa, the "1918 Italian Road Race Champion." Daytona even ran some night races in 1928, as 3,000 fans watched under "lighting arrangements that left something to be desired." Florida also had its share of oval track events. The IMCA's annual visits to the Florida State Fair at Tampa started in 1921. There was a Florida-based circuit in the 1930s that ran at DeLand, Jacksonville, Pompano, Lake City, Cocoa Beach and Tampa.

Top: In 1933 Ray Gast teamed up with the owner of car #2, probably Frank Austin, to head north from Daytona Beach for a race in North Carolina. This rig must have been real fun to tow on the narrow roads of those days. Possibly they were headed for Concord, North Carolina (Bob Gast collection). *Bottom:* The Tampa Florida State Fair races in 1936. Cotton Grable in a Hal is on the pole with Buddy Callaway in his Curtis on the outside. On the outside of row two is West Coast racer, Bayliss Levrett in a Hal (Leverett collection).

Top left: Bob Green of Orlando drove this nice-looking car in 1937. The photograph was probably taken in the Midwest but odds are Green spent his winters racing around home (Wood collection). *Top right:* Promoter Eddie Bland placed this ad in *Illustrated Speedway News* in 1938. Camp Foster was a former Army base near Jacksonville and the races were held on parallel roads. The course was part brick and part dirt and one mile around. *Middle:* Tampa, 1939, and Larry Beckett is shown in his very nice-looking big car. Beckett was an IMCA visitor (Top right and middle photographs—Don Radbruch collection). *Bottom:* NASCAR founder Bill France started his racing career in the big cars. Not too much data is available on his open wheel career, but he was brave enough to race at deadly Lakewood Speedway in Atlanta (Joe Cawley photograph; used with permission from *Auto Racing Memories*).

180 MPH

In 1922 Sig Haugdahl and J. Alex Sloan combined forces to build the Wisconsin Special. It appears that the car was built for an assault on the American land speed record of 156.03 MPH then held by Tommy Milton. Certainly Sloan was also interested in the promotional values such a machine would have for his many dirt track ventures.

The Wisconsin Special was built on the modified chassis of an unknown, but large, passenger car. A very slick body was built with a full belly pan—for the times it was quite advanced. The power plant was a six cylinder 766 cubic inch all aluminum World War I–era aircraft engine. This was called a "Wisconsin" engine—hence the name of the car. Only a few Wisconsin engines were built and it is not known what type of aircraft they were used in.

In April of 1922 the Wisconsin Special was taken to Daytona Beach and Haugdahl drove it to a "world's record" speed of 180.3 MPH. This record was not recognized by the American Automobile Association or any other official record keeping body. Odds are that Sloan didn't really care—he had a "Three Miles per Minute" race car he could hype at his IMCA races.

The Wisconsin Special was probably not actually raced on the dirt tracks, but Haugdahl would run exhibition laps and no doubt climax the act with an attempt to set a "new world's record for a half-mile track." Haugdahl and Sloan's trick stop watch must have set dozens of world records in the early 1920s.

While the dirt track records were pure baloney one has to wonder about the 180 MPH at Daytona. Based on a comparison with other land speed record cars of the era, it *is* possible. Milton's officially recognized American record was made in a car with two Duesenberg racing engines that totaled around 540 cubic inches—aerodynamically this car was similar to the Wisconsin Special. Other reports credit Haugdahl with speeds of 162 and 171 MPH—maybe these were accurate and J. Alex Sloan just liked the nice round number of "three miles per minute." It sold tickets to the dirt track races and that was the name of the game.

Data in a 1978 book—*Speed on Sand*, by Bill Tuthill—does add credence to the Haugdahl record. Tuthill states that the IMCA went to great efforts to insure the accuracy of the Wisconsin Special's record run. The length of the course was surveyed and the timing devices certified before and after the run. The following is quoted from the book, "While that milestone was never recognized by the AAA, a careful check of every bit of information, including eye witnesses, proves that the 180.27 MPH record by Haugdahl was unquestionably authentic."

Racing historian Al Powell of Miami adds some more information that supports the accuracy of Sig Haugdahl's record. In the 1950s Powell drove a race car for H. C. Wilcox. Powell recalls, "We got to talking about Sig Haugdahl and he (Wilcox) told me that they were long time friends. I asked him about the Wisconsin Special and he knew all about the machine. Actually he was at Daytona when Sig ran over 180 MPH and the AAA refused to recognize the mark because Sig was behind on his dues! This is the true fact. Sig argued that he had sent his dues by mail, the AAA

It is believed that these two photographs of the Wisconsin Special were taken in about 1940—obviously at some sort of car show. With those short exhaust pipes the noise of the engine must have been deafening—all the better for Haugdahl to set J. Alex Sloan–type dirt track "world records" (Don Radbruch collection).

said they never got them and asked for another payment. The argument went on and, finally, Sig told them to go to hell, packed his tools, and went back to Jacksonville."

So it appears very likely that Haugdahl did indeed set a world land speed record at Daytona. Is it because J. Alex Sloan manufactured so much hype for so many years that this record has been largely discounted for so long? J. Alex was telling the truth about the "three miles per minute" Wisconsin Special and we didn't believe him!

Top: Sig Haughdahl roars around an unknown dirt track in the early 1920s. Even though the big Wisconsin Special was totally unsuited for a half-mile fairgrounds oval it is obvious that Haugdahl put on one heck of a show! (Christine Horey Logan collection from Grace Jones). *Right:* Sig Haugdahl and the Wisconsin Special at the Florida State Fair in Tampa in about 1922. Haugdahl and the car appeared at countless fairs all over the eastern half of the United States—and probably in Canada (Al Powell collection).

12

Canada
From Sea to Sea

The harsh northern climate and the population density pattern pretty well limit Canadian racing to the southern portion of the country. Allan Brown's *History of America's Speedways—Past and Present* lists several hundred race tracks that have been or are now operating in Canada. Most of the racing has been in recent years

Billy Rogers sits in the driver's seat of a T at Regina, Saskatchewan, in 1915; driver Shorty Youngish is wearing the goggles. There was racing at Regina before this date but Youngish must have competed in other cities to win that impressive lineup of trophies. Leaning on the radiator is Louie Rogers who grew up to be a fine driver (Ralph Rogers collection).

12. Canada 257

and only a few tracks operated before World War II. Early racing has been documented in seven Canadian provinces. Some of this racing was by visiting U.S. drivers, other events combined local and imported racers, and in a few instances the competition was strictly Canadian. Canadian drivers also visited the United States and took home their share of the prize money.

British Columbia had a fair amount of racing in the 1920s and 1930s. This action is summarized in a sidebar by Canadian racing historian Brian Pratt.

Alberta had three known racetracks prior to World War II. Calgary had racing from 1916 to about 1935 at the Calgary Industrial Exhibition. Some, or perhaps all, of these races were stops on the IMCA tour. In Edmon-

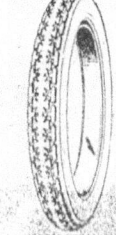

ROY DUSANG WINS

The Challenge Race for $1,000 Purse on

"GUTTA PERCHA" TIRES
(CROSS-TREAD)

Dusang Said, "My Only Hope, Gutta Percha Tires, as I Did Not Skid So Much."

BUY
"Gutta Percha" Tires
NOW!

To be had at all up-to-the-minute dealers

Right: A 1920s ad in a Canadian publication. Great name for a tire! While "gutta-percha" may sound like pidgin Italian for "good purchase" (traction), it is actually the rubber-like gum used in golf ball cores. *Below:* It is probable that this photograph was taken in Canada but the exact location is unknown. Dave Koetzla is shown at the wheel of his Essex bobtail. Koetzla is best remembered as the manager of Gilmore Stadium in the 1930s and '40s, but he spent his youth on the IMCA dirt tracks (Both photographs—Tom Saal collection).

Top: Emory Collins in his Chevy in about 1925. Collins was a Canadian and got his start on the dusty ovals of Alberta and Saskatchewan (Dave Norgaarden collection). *Middle:* Most likely someplace in Saskatchewan and in the mid–1920s. Louie Rogers' Model T has an OHC head built by the family's Rogers Machine Works. *Bottom:* This is Louie Rogers' street hot rod/race car. It is believed that this car had a homemade overhead-cam engine (Lower photographs—Ralph Rogers collection).

ton there was racing on an intermittent basis from 1916 until 1935 at a track that might have been called Breckenridge Speedway. Lethbridge had one race in about 1926.

In Saskatchewan racing began at Regina at some point prior to 1915 and continued, perhaps annually, until 1937—much of this was under IMCA sanction. Saskatoon had racing in 1917, 1918 and around 1926. There was also racing at Semans on a half-mile oval in 1920 and 1921.

Manitoba racing was at Brandon in 1917, 1918 and in the mid-1920s. The only other action was at Winnipeg where the IMCA ran from 1915 until 1925 with another race in 1936. Portage La Prairie hosted one race in 1920.

Toronto in Ontario had racing in 1904 at the Canadian National Expo. This racing resumed in 1917 and lasted until 1934—it is known that the IMCA raced there from 1920 to 1928. Ottawa had racing in 1917 and 1918 but things were then quiet until Ralph Hankinson brought in AAA drivers in 1934 and 1935.

Other Ontario racing was apparently on a very intermittent basis at towns like Chatham, Essex. Leamington, Norwood and Sarnia. In the mid-1920s there was racing at what is today the Thunder Bay area. Tracks at Fort William and Murillo attracted American visitors who raced against the locals. Of interest in Ontario is a one-mile track at Fort Erie, near Niagara Falls, which hosted perhaps the first auto race in Canada on September 19, 1901.

Action at Hastings Park in Vancouver in about 1927. Note the small car at the right of those lined up on the rail. Isolated midgets show up at all sorts of places long before their official debut in 1933 (Brian Pratt collection).

Quebec provides a Canadian mystery as, apparently, the only early racing in that huge and populous province was in 1917 and 1918. This was at Deslormiers Park in Montreal and at Quebec City. There just has to be some missing racing history in Quebec.

On Canada's east coast there was at least one race held in Nova Scotia. This was at the Halifax Exhibition Track on October 3, 1936.

Top: Colwood Park near Victoria in about 1927. Left to right are Phil Foster, Ed Allen, Jack Smith and George Lapp. Foster's and Lapp's machines are really street hot rods or track roadsters (McMurtry collection; photograph by Johnny Wright). *Bottom:* This is a 1920 ad for races at the Willows Track north of Victoria on Vancouver Island. Over the years other ads promised that the track "Will be dustless." Wonder if it ever was? (Brian Pratt collection).

Top: The Willows on May 25, 1934. Veteran Mario Bianchi, at the left, was nearing the end of a long and successful career. At the right a young Jimmy Wilburn sits in his car—one of the first races of his career. *Bottom:* Another view of the Bianchi and Wilburn cars at The Willows. Despite the huge crowd on hand the purse was pegged at $400 (Both photographs—McMurtry collection).

Top: Phil Foster drove the Johnny Wright Special in the 1935 race at The Willows. *Middle:* Not much is known about this car at the 1935 Willows race. What on earth is a Baby Miller? *Bottom:* Jack Smith's car at The Willows. Smith had a long and illustrious career as a Canadian car builder (All photographs—McMurtry collection).

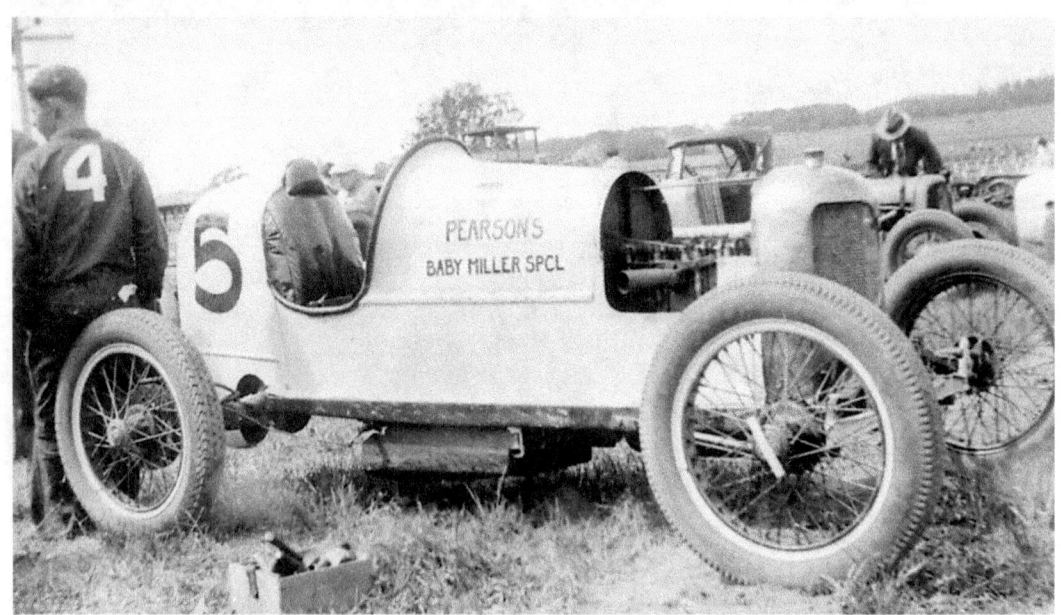

Top: Jimmy Wilburn in action at Langford Speedway in Victoria in 1936. Note the loose oiled dirt surface and the many stones. For obvious reasons the track was soon paved. *Bottom:* Jimmy Wilburn scoots into the lead on opening day at Langford. The large crowd was soon coated with oily dust (Both photographs — McMurtry collection).

Top: Things were a bit unfinished when Langford opened in 1936. This looks like warmups are just about to get underway (McMurtry collection). *Bottom:* It rains a lot in British Columbia, and Langford Speedway briefly tried a "rain or shine" racing policy. It is doubtful if the drivers liked it and apparently neither did the spectators. Jack Spaulding jumps into the lead (Pike Green collection).

Top: Looks like the start of a heat race at Langford. Tony West tries to beat Swede Lindskog into the first turn as Bert Bloomgren and Jack Spaulding follow. Lindskog soon moved to Los Angeles and starred at Gilmore Stadium. The other drivers stayed home and did well in both the big cars and midgets (Bill Hill collection). *Right:* Lew McMurtry was one of the Seattle-area drivers who made regular trips to race at Langford Speedway. Here he is shown in the Al Hanson Fronty T (McMurtry collection). *Bottom:* Action at Langford Speedway on opening day. With all those rocks flying around, Jimmy Wilburn, on the outside, gives an unidentified driver lots of room (McMurtry collection; photograph by Johnny Wright).

Big Cars in British Columbia

Almost all of the racing in British Columbia was in the province's major cities of Victoria and Vancouver. Vancouver had most of its racing in the 1920s, while the 1930s were Victoria's era.

Most of the action in Vancouver was at Hastings Park. The half-mile horse track was used for auto racing as early as 1907 with fairly frequent events beginning in 1918. Seattle promoter Robert Hiller (aka Hillier) brought up a field of Seattle- and Tacoma-based cars for a July 1, 1918, meet. It was a success and a second meet followed in conjunction with the annual late summer Vancouver Exhibition, starting a tradition that would continue until 1927.

Drivers appearing at Hastings Park over the years included Gus Duray, George Lott, Tip Bloom, and Jack Ross. The hot setup started out to be the Stutz but it didn't take too long for the Fronty Fords to start winning races. Of interest was the Romano Special of E. Jean Romano—it had a V-8 Curtiss aircraft engine stuffed in a tiny white racer. This car won the first Pikes Peak race.

Most races were sanctioned by northwest associations that fell under the AAA umbrella, but there was a blip from the norm in 1920 when the IMCA sanctioned the races during the Exhibition. An inter-association race, complete with wagers, was the highlight of these races. Jack Ross, for the AAA, won the ten-mile duel over the IMCA's Fred Horey but only after Horey's Essex broke down. In 1926 the Hastings Park races featured a group advertised as the "California Dirt Track Kings." Included among the drivers were Al Hopp, Jimmy Sharp and Francis Quinn.

Two fatalities at Hastings Park had long-term effects. In 1923 local driver Dudley Smith was killed during the Exhibition races. The result of an inquest was to limit the number of local entries in future races, as these drivers were deemed not to have enough experience to compete with the more competent American visitors. In 1927 a bad multi-car wreck left Seattle driver Phil Churchill dead. Again, this occurred during the Vancouver Exhibition races. Probably as a result of this second fatality there were no more Exhibition races until 1937—and that was an indoor midget race.

Across the Strait of Georgia, at Victoria on Vancouver Island, the 1920s and '30s saw a handful of races at The Willows—a half-mile fairground track. In 1919 and 1920 events featured the usual Seattle cars and drivers but a bit later on local drivers like Jack Smith and Phil Foster were featured. (Foster's nephew, Billy, became the first Canadian driver to compete at Indianapolis.) In 1934 the British Columbia Automotive Sports Association (BCASA) was formed and held races at Nanaimo and on a mile horse track at Colwood near Victoria. A 1935 race at the Willows resulted in Jimmy Wilburn and Mario Bianchi running away from locals Phil Foster and Johnny Wright, but the trend of ferrying cars had begun. This practice really got going when BCASA efforts resulted in the building of Langford Speedway in 1936.

An interesting bit of reminiscence by Johnny Wright in *National Speed Sport News* in 1951, after Langford had been sold, gave an account of the track's beginning:

Langford Speedway was built in 1936 on property owned by racing enthusiast Jack Taylor. Clay was hauled in, gallons of old crankcase oil poured into the recipe, and there was the track, as loose as a goose with millions of big rocks just waiting to be tossed up by the flying wheels. To make the plant perfect a set of bleachers was erected and a board fence wrapped around the deal—all ready for the grand opening. On opening day, all the city bigwigs were invited and with their ladies fair, all dressed in spotless white, they were given the preference of ringside seats. Well, the results were self explanatory. The local dry cleaners had a bumper week and, before long, the track was paved.

Langford Speedway benefited from the midgets' coming to the Pacific Northwest. Vancouver went the midget route. With no regular big car track south of the border, almost weekly "International Auto Races" were run at Langford through the 1941 season. Lasting friendships were established, parts exchanged (aka smuggled?), cars brought, bottles stuck up straight pipes, and probably nothing was declared except, "Let's do it again soon." And they did, the next season after the war was over.

This section was written by Brian Pratt of Burnaby, British Columbia.

Strange Shenanigans in Saskatchewan

Three-time Indy winner Lou Meyer was a versatile driver and posted wins not only on the bricks but on the boards, on dirt and in stock cars. Would you believe he even won a tractor race?

The story is reported in the Regina, Saskatchewan, newspaper on August 3, 1934. Just what Meyer was doing on the Canadian prairie and how he was talked into racing a tractor is not related in the story, but here's what happened.

It was a six-lap race with three tractors, and at halfway the drivers had to stop and put on a pair of overalls. Meyer was running last at the end of the third lap and his competitors, "determined to put the Indy Speed King to shame," playfully threw Meyer's overalls over the fence and into the stands. Undaunted, Meyer retrieved the overalls, put them on, and jumped onto a special tractor that just happened to be standing nearby. This machine was capable of speeds up to 70 MPH so Meyer quickly made up ground, caught the other two tractors, and won the race in dramatic fashion.

Did the AAA know about this escapade—or did their dictatorial control of drivers not extend to tractors?

On the Docks

The transportation method used to get U.S. cars to races in Victoria, British Columbia, provided a unique photo opportunity. Victoria is on Vancouver Island and accessible only by ferry. Upon arrival in that city there were a few minutes avail-

Top: July 18, 1939: Race cars waiting to be towed to Langford. *Bottom:* 1939: Jerry Vanteight and a rare early roll bar—and a rare Nash engine (Both photographs—Pike Green collection.)

Top: Jimmy Seim's car. *Bottom:* Jimmy Laird drove this nice-looking car (Both photographs—Pike Green collection).

able to relax while waiting for Canadian friends to tow the race cars to Langford Speedway—U.S. racers usually left their passenger cars on the docks in Seattle. Numerous photos were taken on the docks in Victoria—some of these are presented below.

(All photographs are from the Pike Green collection).

Top: Swede Lindskog in 1939. *Bottom:* This is the Bob Bailey Miller–Schofield (Both photographs—Pike Green collection).

Top: This must be on the way home—looks like this car got upside down. *Bottom:* An unknown car. This photograph was taken at Phil Foster's Esso Station in Victoria—another popular photo-taking spot (Both photographs—Pike Green collection).

The Midday Ride of Wes Moore

Foremost among the fun racing of the late 1930s were the events at Langford Speedway in Victoria, British Columbia. The races, usually on Saturday nights, attracted a sizeable contingent of cars from the Seattle area. This meant a four-hour trip on the Canadian Pacific Railroad ferry boat—ships that made only two trips per day. For the racers the 9 A.M. ferry was the most convenient—the 1 P.M. arrival gave plenty of time to get to the race track north of Victoria. The ferry was expensive so the economy-minded (i.e. usually broke) racers would leave their passenger cars at the dock and push the race car loaded with tools and spares, on to the ferry. At the Victoria end there was no shortage of Canadian volunteers to give them a lift to the track and tow the race car on a rope.

Wes Moore of Seattle made many trips to Langford, but one race in August of 1937 turned out to be more than routine. During the running of the feature race that night at Langford his Hal broke an axle and lost both the wheel and axle. After the races the normal festivities began and that was no time for Moore to worry about fixing his race car.

When Sunday morning dawned, Wes and a few equally bleary-eyed helpers set

Wes Moore is pictured at Phil Foster's Esso Station in Victoria, a popular hangout for visiting American racers. This is probably the same car that Moore used to set a somewhat unofficial Langford Speedway-to-the-ferry-docks record a couple of years earlier (Pike Green collection).

about finding the parts and making the necessary repairs—the last ferry of the day left at 4 P.M. It took considerable time to round up the necessary parts and it was well into the afternoon when the crew started to put the Hal together under a blazing sun at Langford Speedway. Obviously, it was going to be close making the deadline set by the ferry departure.

Finally the last bolt was tightened with only a bit over 20 minutes left to tow the car 15 miles through the center of Victoria—they'd never make the ferry. Wes Moore had the solution. Firing up the Hal he took off down the crowded two-lane highway towards the city center. Fortunately the Hal had a clutch and transmission, so this helped to negotiate the heavy Sunday traffic. Just as fortunately the police lacked the refined communications systems that would doom such a ride today—they could only give chase to the speeding race car. Moore roared through the center of Victoria to the docks, and in a manner well suited to a Hollywood thriller, raced down the loading ramp just as it was being raised. Moore was safely on the ship to the cheers of friends and onlookers. As the ship faded into the afternoon sun the few police who had bothered to keep up the chase stood on the dock with mixed feelings of irritation and admiration.

Moore's wild ride was written up in a good-natured newspaper article the following day. The Victoria police were quick to forgive the whole thing and no charges were filed against Wes Moore. It is no wonder the good times at Langford were long remembered!

Thanks to Pike Green of Mesa, Arizona, for information on this tale.

13

Those Pesky Midgets

When they came on the racing scene in 1933 it didn't take long for the midgets to affect the full size race cars. As related elsewhere in the book, the effect was negative—the big cars were soon hurting at the box office.

The midgets ran exhibition races against the big cars as early as 1934, but they were not competitive with the larger and more powerful machines. The first record of midgets actually competing with the big cars was in the summer of 1936.

This racing was nicely documented by George Sparks in a story in *Coast Auto Racing* called "A Race Driver's Diary." A half-dozen midgets from Los Angeles headed towards the Midwest on a barnstorming trip. Starting in Colorado, most of the races were on makeshift tracks around baseball fields. Somehow, the sparse field put on crowd pleasing shows. In Kansas the midgets ran several races of their own and then went up against the big cars on half-mile ovals at Anthony and Eureka. The results were surprising—the midgets easily beat the big cars and won both main events. It must be remembered that author Sparks was driving a midget and could be a bit prejudiced, but he does document the time trials at Anthony. The midgets were one to two seconds faster than the four big cars present. The quality of the big car competition is not known but one of the drivers was Waldo Barnett—a better-than-average competitor. The midgets that made the long journey were not the top cars from Los Angeles. They were probably class B machines, although drivers like D. W. McCauley, Louis Durant and Harry Hart were behind the steering wheels.

A more notable battle between the midgets and big cars took place at the one-

Opposite top: "Hey, ain't this thing cute?" is what Stubby Stubblefield seems to be saying as he sits in Harry Alley's midget. This was at Oakland Speedway in early 1933. "Cute" or not, Alley has a major sponsor—the Nehi Company was a leading West Coast soft-drink bottler. *Bottom:* Racing legend Wilbur Shaw is shown in Ken Brenneman's street-legal midget at Oakland in 1933. The driver at the left is Brenneman and that's Bryan Saulpaugh at the right. Certainly, these drivers did not take such a machine seriously (Both photographs—Bruce Craig collection).

Top: Mel Hansen is shown in the Snyder Offy at a southern California track in 1936. Hansen journeyed northward to Oakland and helped Pat Cunningham humiliate the big cars in a hundred-mile race (Jerry Trueblood collection). *Middle:* Pat Cunningham in the Fayte Brown Offy at Oakland Speedway on November 8, 1936. Mel Hansen's ride sits in the next pit apparently undergoing a temporary number change. It seems likely that the unknown photographer would have taken some action shots on that day but the photos could not be found (Craig-Alvarez collection from Jerry Trueblood). *Bottom:* The Offys at Oakland made headlines in the *National Auto Racing News*. This was the leading auto racing publication in 1936, and as *National Speed Sport News*, it still is (Used with the permission of *NSSN* and Chris Economaki).

mile banked Oakland Speedway on November 8, 1936. A couple of Offy midgets, driven by Pat Cunningham and Mel Hansen, were invited to compete in a hundred-mile big car race. These midgets, and their drivers, were among the best in the nation. Excellent documentation for this race is available in a *National Auto Racing News* headline article by Jack Carmody, supplemented—for what it is worth—by my own memories of the race.

In the time trials Bud Rose in a Miller was fastest at 39.20 seconds and Fred Agabashian second at 39.80—Mel Hansen, in one of the Offys, was third at 40.01. In the hundred-miler there were but thirteen starters as Bud Rose jumped into an early lead. He was quickly challenged by Mel Hansen—Rose was faster on the straightaways but the nimble midget more than made up ground on the turns. Meanwhile Pat Cunningham was coasting along in fourth place. Cunningham slowly picked up the pace and by the 40th-mile was in the lead. Hansen had to make the first of two fuel stops and shortly thereafter Rose was forced to slow his pace with mechanical problems. From that point on, Pat Cunningham cruised to an easy win. He averaged a respectable 83.78 MPH, and at the end of 100 miles held a five-lap lead over Mel Hansen. Rose held on for third but was eight miles in arrears, and Swede Lindskog finished fourth some 13 miles back.

It was a lousy show, but the midgets made it interesting for the 5,000 fans and Jack Carmody wrote a quite positive *National Auto Racing News* story on the race. For me, at age 12, racing could do no wrong—it was marvelous! Local sportswriter Alan Ward had different thoughts and summed it up the next day in the *Oakland Tribune*, "Lined up with the midgets were eleven fugitives from the speedway junk pile." Ward was normally a friend of racing!

There was no way the midgets would have been competitive with a top-notch field of AAA big cars. When the AAA ran at Oakland a few years earlier, their Millers were three to ten seconds faster than the Bud Rose Miller and the other cars present on that day. After the race the Oakland Speedway management announced that there would be another hundred-miler a month later and ten Offy midgets would be on hand. This race never happened. (The midgets did run their own 150-mile races on the Oakland Mile in 1937 and 1938.)

There were other instances of midgets running against and beating the big cars, but the Oakland race was the high point of this competition. Oakland proved that good midgets could beat second-rate big cars even on a mile track. In his *NARN* article Jack Carmody wrote, "Just what effect the victory of the midget cars over big cars will have on local racing is problematical. If the racing public considers the little cars toys, as a few still do, the big cars will suffer in public esteem. If the average fan accepts the midgets for what they really are—high class bundles of real racing machinery—then possibly the game is reaching a new and healthy state of life."

The main reason for the 1936 midget vs. big car racing was the shortage of cars. Any promotional advantage for the big cars quickly soured. The midgets proved they weren't toys and the big cars got the message that they'd better stick to their own races.

14

The Way It Was

The First Racing Publication?

It is probable that *Speedway Magazine* was the first auto-racing publication. The December 1932 issue pictured here is Volume 1, Number 5; hence the first issue must have been in mid–1932. (*National Speed Sport News* began life as one page of New Jersey's *Bargain Herald* in the summer of 1932, but was not a separate publication (as *National Auto Racing News* until 1934.)

Speedway Magazine was published monthly by Ralph Ormsby Jr. in Cincinnati, Ohio, and was a first-class publication with excellent photographs. Much of the coverage was on Indy and Legion Ascot but there was some local material from various parts of the country and several regular columnists. There was even a bit of overseas news and some feature stories on drivers. For the times it was expensive—25 cents per copy and $2.00 for 12 issues per year.

Copies of *Speedway Magazine* are extremely rare so it must not have lasted long.

Cover of *Speedway Magazine*, December 1932 (Roy Eaton collection).

National Speed Sport News—The War Years

The leading auto racing newspaper in the years prior to World War II was the *National Auto Racing News*. It suspended publication shortly after wartime regulations resulted in the ban on all auto racing on July 31, 1942. Publication was resumed in February 1943 as *National Speed Sport News*, and this weekly newspaper is still going strong today.

National Speed Sport News was published monthly from 1943 until the war was over in September 1945. With no current racing to fill the pages NSSN called upon dedicated columnists to rehash old races and report on the whereabouts of drivers and owners now in the service. Photos from the past were printed and the publication kept the sport alive during the dark days of the war. Servicemen in the far-flung corners of the globe particularly treasured the "news from home" as reported by *NSSN*.

In addition to the monthly newspaper, *NSSN* published an annual "Foto Review" in 1943, 1944 and 1945. These were slick paper magazine-type publications full of photos of racing in days past. The price was all of one dollar including postage!

The cover of the *NSSN*'s "Foto Review."

Some of the photos from the 1943 and 1945 issues are reproduced below. The quality of the photos is remarkably good considering the printing technology of the 1940s. Captions were a bit sparse and sometimes incorrect—some of these have been expanded on a bit or corrected. This material is used with the permission of Chris Economake of *National Speed Sport News*.

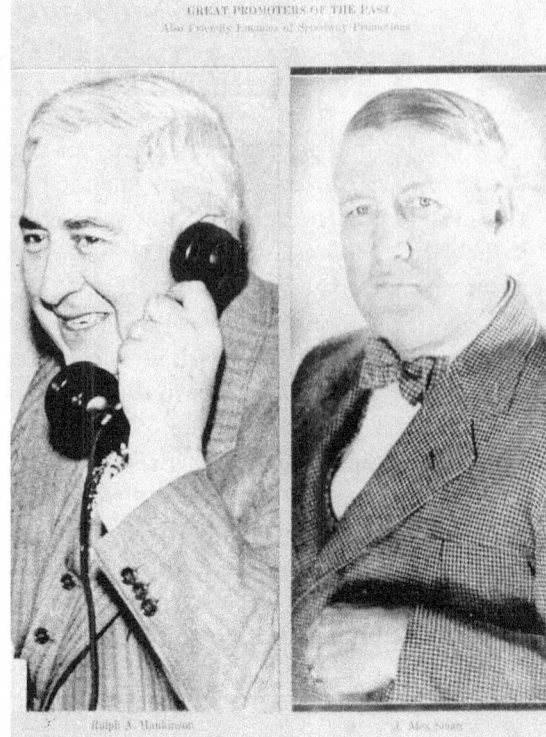

Right: The 1943 "Foto Review" paid tribute to two of the greatest prewar promoters. *Below:* This Clarksburg, West Virginia, photograph was taken in about 1935.

A large crowd was on hand for the opening of the Hammond, Indiana, race track in 1937. As the bottom photograph shows, at least three race cars wound up in the adjacent dump on that day.

Top: Jimmy Wilburn gets a trophy from Frank Funk at Winchester in about 1938. Funk was famous (notorious?) for his tiny trophies. *Middle:* Cecil Yates drove this unusual-looking car at an unknown track. *Bottom:* The field lines up at Oklahoma City—probably in the mid–1930s.

Top: Both issues of "Foto Review" had coverage of races held at Parana, Argentina, in about 1932. The 1931 Indy winner, Lou Schneider, was on hand with what looks to be a 1928–29 Indy Miller. Schneider was among several American stars who appeared in South American races in the 1930s—it is not known how they fared. *Bottom:* This is Leamington—not Lamington.

Best of the 1930s

Arguably, the 1930s produced some of the best race drivers of the century. These were drivers who raced not only at Indianapolis but at dirt tracks all over the United States. Most of these drivers appear in other photographs elsewhere in this book, but this is an exceptional group of photos. All were taken from 1933 to 1935 either at Oakland Speedway or at Legion Ascot in California. The photographer is unknown but it might have been Ted Wilson. They are from the collection of Lew

Lewis of Live Oak, California. Lewis got them from a friend who is a distant descendent of Frank Hood, the AAA Zone Supervisor for Northern California in the 1930s. Unlike some AAA Zone Supervisors, Hood was popular with the drivers and most of the photos are autographed to him.

Left: Chet Gardner. *Below:* Stubby Stubblefield (Both photographs—Lew Lewis collection).

Top: Babe Stapp. *Middle right:* Lou Schneider. *Middle left:* Billy Winn. *Bottom:* Wilbur Shaw (All photographs—Lew Lewis collection).

Top left: **Mauri Rose.** *Top right:* Left to right, **Bob Carey, Bryan Saulpaugh, Wilbur Shaw.** *Middle:* **Lou Meyer.** *Bottom:* **Harris Insinger** (All photographs—Lew Lewis collection).

Top: Rex Mays. *Right:* Bill Cummings. *Bottom:* Floyd Roberts with Ronnie Parent. *Left:* Ernie Triplett (All photographs—Lew Lewis collection).

Lady Racers

With all the hype that accompanied many of the early auto races it is logical that women would be a part of this promotional tool. It is probable that dozens of women took part in exhibition races and/or performed stunts of various kinds. Unfortunately most of these brave souls have been long forgotten, but the careers of several women can, to a small extent, be documented.

Two of them, Lillian Boyer and Gladys Roy, executed airplane stunts in conjunction with auto races or at air shows. Roy apparently did a wing walking act that concluded with some form of tennis played on the top wing of a biplane. Gladys Roy was killed, not during a stunt, but when she walked into the propeller of an airplane on the ground. Lillian Boyer accomplished a racing-car-to-aircraft change on the main straightaway of race tracks in front of crowded grandstands. Ms. Boyer survived this dangerous stunt at St. Paul, Minnesota, and Huron, South Dakota, as did the nearby crowds. Aviation officials soon put a stop to auto-airplane changes at fairgrounds venues. Lillian Boyer married race driver Swan Peterson and, presumably, lived happily ever after in California.

Other women actually drove race cars. The races were exhibition runs against time or match races with male drivers. Elfrieda Mais was a well-known and obviously capable driver who graced promotions (often put on by J. Alex Sloan) from Alabama to Massachusetts to Montana and Canada. She started her career in 1910 and won her title as the "World's Fastest Woman" in 1915. Among her accomplishments was defeating Louis Disbrow in a match race at Toronto in 1924—hippodrome or not, obviously drove fast. She was killed at Birmingham, Alabama, in 1934 when a flaming-wall stunt, complete with exploding dynamite, went awry.

Joan LaCosta was another female racer hyped by Sloan. She reportedly went 143.4 MPH in a speed trial at Jacksonville Beach in Florida. On oval tracks she routinely broke existing women's lap records by up to ten seconds. It is a wonder that Sloan didn't match La Costa and Mais in a big race.

Dorothy Walker drove at Overland Park in Denver around 1926. She was the young wife of driver A. J. Walker and was billed as the "Masked Marvel." Perhaps the sum total of her racing career is listed in the results of the day's races: "Fifth Race. Five Mile Exhibition by Masked Marvel. Race halted when the accident occurred in which Mrs. Dorothy Walker was killed."

Elfrieda Mais in about 1925 (Photograph from *Auto Racing Memories;* used with permission from Ken Breslauer).

Top: Elfrieda Mais in a bobtail at an unknown location. From the cars in the background it must be the mid–1920s (Bruce Craig collection from Bob Lawrence). *Bottom:* Elfrieda Mais performs her burning-wall stunt at Ionia, Michigan, in 1934. During the peak of the fair season Ms. Mais probably did this three or four times a week (Christine Horey Logan collection from Grace Jones).

The wall crash by Elfrieda Mais provided some spectacular action as shown here. Usually the wall was on fire and sometimes dynamite exploded at the moment of the crash (Christine Horey Logan collection from Grace Jones).

The National Championship Drivers of America

The mid-1930s were lean years for Indy-car racing. Other than the annual 500-mile race at Indianapolis there were only a few events that carried points for the AAA National Championship. The purses for these events were small even by the standards of the day.

In the summer of 1935 the top AAA drivers got together and organized themselves as the National Championship Drivers of America (NCDA). The plan was to promote races themselves and thus get a bigger portion of the gate receipts. Races for the two-man Indy cars would be held on suitable one-mile dirt tracks throughout the nation. Among the drivers participating in the venture were Floyd Roberts, Rex Mays, Lou Meyer, Lou Moore, Chet Gardner, Babe Stapp, Bill Cummings, Wilbur Shaw, Fred Frame, Al Gordon and Shorty Cantlon. Missing from the list was an important name for 1935—Kelly Petillo.

To help NCDA work, all the drivers agreed to forgo any appearance money—they'd all race for what they got. Kelly Petillo, as the 1935 Indy winner, demanded appearance money—the amount is long forgotten. Petillo was an obnoxious character before his Indy win—afterwards, he was insufferable. Perhaps, had it been anybody but Petillo, a deal could have been worked out. NCDA had to go on without the Indy winner. The group's promotions were not successful and a series of rained out events did not help.

The NCDA drivers did run a couple of races at Ascot and one at Oakland in California. These were AAA-sanctioned and the "self-promoting" aspect of NCDA apparently was not in effect. One Ascot race attracted over 20,000 fans but the purse, split evenly among eleven cars, was only $2,200.

The National Championship Drivers of American was disbanded early in the year 1936.

Creative Financing

Earl Mansell of Santa Maria, California, remembers that racing in the early 1930s was just like today, "You couldn't make it on the purses—you had to have a sponser to help pay the bills." Sponsers were tough to come by in those Depression years, but Mansell found a unique solution that helped him buy and maintain a Fronty race car in 1933.

Prohibition was in effect in 1933. This was certainly the most unpopular and widely ignored law in history. Bootleg (illegal) liquor was easily obtainable and it seemed that everybody had their own bootlegger.

Earl Mansell had a friend, Harry Clark, who was active in the bootlegging business. He entered into a partnership with Clark by hauling grain alcohol in his innocent-appearing Model A Ford roadster. Earl recalls, "I had a special spring on the back and we could carry ten five-gallon cans in the rumble seat space. We bought the alcohol wholesale at $8.00 a gallon and I hauled it to downtown San Diego where we'd set up a whiskey-making operation in the grease pit of a garage. We'd put the alcohol, some water, and flavoring of some sort in a big oak barrel. Clark would hook up

Earl Mansell is shown at Silvergate Speedway, San Diego, in 1934. This is not the car that Mansell financed with sales of illegal booze (Rod Eschenburg collection).

some wires and run a 110-volt current through the mixture overnight. The next day we had whiskey we'd advertise as being 16 years old. We called it Panther Piss and even had labels printed for the bottles."

The illegal, but popular, operation paid for the Fronty which Mansell raced for a time on a Pacific Coast and then headed east. Panther Piss must have been good stuff as Harry Clark continued to manufacture the whiskey even after prohibition was repealed in mid–1933. He then ran afoul of the law and spent some time in jail. Mansell was racing in the Midwest and out of harm's way. No, the Panther Piss logo was not on the race car.

Mansell raced from 1925 until 1951 and competed at legendary Legion Ascot Speedway. He was a car owner after World War II and his sprinter, with Hank Henry driving, finished second in a 500-mile race at Riverside Raceway in California in 1951.

Deal Money

Odds are that in much of today's racing any arrangement we could call "deal money" starts out, "My lawyer will call your lawyer." It wasn't that way in the 1930s. From Earl Mansell comes information on how things worked.

Earl competed at Legion Ascot Speedway in the early 1930s. He got to know Gus Schrader when Gus journeyed westward to try his luck at Ascot. Earl was interested in running in the Midwest with the IMCA so Schrader set up a deal with J. Alex Sloan for the next summer.

Mansell headed east from his San Diego home in late May of 1934 and ran a number of IMCA events for a guarantee of $150 per race. He remembers that "A lot of the races were what we called barnstorming races (hippodromes) and my job was to finish third behind Gus and Emory Collins. They seemed to take turns winning. Heck, I wasn't going to beat those guys anyhow with my Fronty T."

While running the IMCA circuit Mansell met promoter Max Jacobs from Jackson, Michigan, who needed cars for any upcoming race. Mansell and a couple of other drivers were offered a guarantee of $200 to race at Jackson. "You met people, found out about races and just went there," Mansell recalls. "After Jackson I went to places like Joliet and Mazon in Illinois. At Mazon it was so dusty that I quit and was lucky enough to find my way to the infield—all the other cars crashed."

Earl Mansell was quick to point out that he raced because he wanted to and not for money. Money driver or not he did OK and made some good deals in 1934. (Better than I did in 1953 when I ran with IMCA—we got $75 per race.)

Hippodrome

The word "hippodrome" comes from the Greek—hippos, horse plus dromos, course. It is defined as an arena for sports and games. Just how it became a racing term for a fake or staged race is unknown. Maybe because an awful lot of hippodromed races took place on "horse courses?"

The first hippodromed races probably took place when Barney Oldfield was racing Lincoln Beachy in his primitive airplane. Although the races were not necessarily fixed, clearly the goal was to "make it look close." (There are reports that the two took turns winning.)

Racing is show biz and the object is to put on a good show for the spectators. If one or two cars run away from everybody it is a lousy show. If the faster cars slow down a bit and dice with each other as the field closes up it is a good show. Early promoters were quick to recognize this—especially since they usually did not have a really competitive field.

Hippodroming was common in the 1920s and 1930s. There was not only the "put on a good show" aspect, but often track conditions were just too dangerous to race at full speed. On other occasions, the promotion would sour and the crowd would be scant—put on a show and come back another day.

The most famous hippodroming circuit was the IMCA. At most of the bigger fairs, like the state fairs, the IMCA races were on the up and up and the drivers raced hard for the money. The smaller fairs were the backbone of the IMCA schedule and these were routinely hippodromed. There was not necessarily a designated winner, but rather an unwritten rule that the fastest qualifier would win the feature race. This really didn't make much difference as the IMCA usually had one or two dominant drivers who would win anyhow.

When some of the smaller racing groups hippodromed a race the payoff was the same for everybody. In the IMCA there were set payoffs depending on how good the driver and/or his car was. Numbers are hard to come by, but drivers like Gus Schrader and Emory Collins are rumored to have received up to $400 per race.

Does hippodroming occur today? Some strange things seem to happen in certain major stock car races. Maybe a bit of "Let's make it look close?"

I do not mean to demean the skills of drivers who took part in hippodromed races. It took a lot of courage, experience and savvy to "put on a show" at even 90 percent of full speed.

Real Dollars

The payoffs for winning races before World War II seem minuscule compared to the big numbers today's drivers take home. The value of a dollar has changed more over the years than we sometimes realize. No need to go into a detailed comparison of the

```
   Quick Service         25¢         Well Cooked
         Complete Plate Lunch
                      Consisting of
              One of three kinds of Meat, Potatoes,
    Two Kinds of Vegetables              Home Made Pie
                    Coffee, Tea or Milk
                           also
             Steak or Chop Supper
    with Potatoes    Two kinds of Vegetables    Home Made Pie
                    Tea, Coffee or Milk, for
                          25¢
              Pink Pig Lunch
    Southwest corner of 2nd avenue and "F" street
    Ice Cold Beer                         Clean Food
```

An ad from a 1934 Silvergate Speedway program (Rod Eschenburg collection).

economy then and now—this ad from a 1934 Silvergate Speedway (San Diego) program says it all.

Medical Aid

Most of us who raced long ago seem to take pleasure in criticizing today's racing. We don't like the wide tires, drivers who are hidden from view by incredibly ugly sprint car bodies and wings, and the fact that chassis preparation diminishes the importance of the driver *driving* the car. We cannot, however, fault the wonderful medical attention available at modern race tracks.

The man in the center appears to be fanning this injured driver. That's racer Mel Kenealy at the right (Eckert collection from Pike Green).

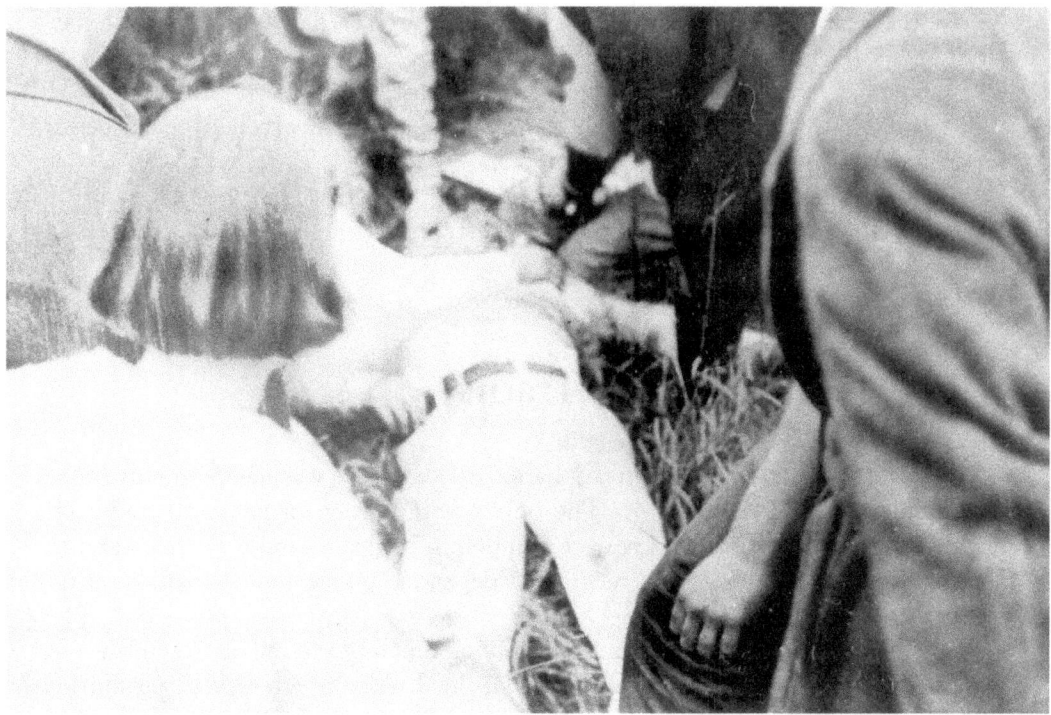

Willing, but certainly untrained, people attend to this injured driver—let's hope that he was OK (Eckert collection from Pike Green).

Needless to say it wasn't always that way. Many races were run without an ambulance being present. At one eastern race in about 1930 a driver was seriously injured—internal injuries and two broken legs. He was taken to the hospital laid out on the folds of the canvas top of a Model A roadster, with two men holding him in place by standing on the running boards. There are reports of drivers being refused admittance to hospitals because the promoter hadn't paid the bills from the last driver who was hurt. Medical personnel at race tracks were untrained in handling an injured driver. There is no denying that racing was much more dangerous before the advent of roll cages, but was poor first aid procedures added to this toll.

My own experience provides a further illustration. In 1948 I went over the ten-foot bank at Watsonville, California, in a track roadster. During the car's wild gyrations it landed hard upside down and I was driven down into the seat of the roadster. The car finally landed right side up, and after a short time help arrived. I told them my back hurt—a backboard and a helicopter ride to the hospital? Watsonville in 1948—yeah sure! Pit crewmen helped me out of the wrecked car and helped me walk up the bank to the ambulance. A doctor was on hand here and he made me lie down. Since I could move various parts of me I was not taken to the hospital until after the races. There X-rays were taken and the doctor looked at them and said, "You'd better lie down, you have a broken back." It turned out that I hurt in one place, and the possible cracked vertebra on the X-ray was in another place. Further

X-rays the next day indicated that there was no vertebra damage—I guess it was a strain of some kind and it hurt like hell for a few weeks.

Though I received reasonably good care for the time, drivers of the 1920s and 1930s would have found less medical attention available. The excellent trackside care found today is a great advance for the sport.

It is probably for the better, but photos of injured drivers in the 1920s and '30s are rare. Photographers were discouraged, restrained is a better word, from taking such pictures.

Trains

In the 1920s Interstate highways barely existed. This was one reason most racing groups stayed close to home. The only practical way for racers to travel long distances was by train. Race cars were shipped in baggage cars or box cars and the comfort level of the drivers and mechanics depended on the budget—chair car or a Pullman.

As recorded in various sections of the book much of the racing in remote areas was by traveling groups of cars and drivers. the J. Alex Sloan IMCA promotions reached the far corners of the United States as well as up into Canada. There is evidence that Sloan used private trains to transport his roving group of racers. This may or may not be true. One problem is that Mr. Sloan was prone to use a bit of ballyhoo in his promotions. Were the "private trains" more Sloan hype?

Research on the train travel of the 1920s extended to the National Railway Museum in Philadelphia. The museum personnel had no specific knowledge of auto racing but they did apply their general knowledge of railroad history. They felt that private trains were used only by large traveling organizations like circuses or Buffalo Bill's Wild West Show. It would almost certainly be too expensive for somebody like Sloan to transport a dozen race cars, some support vehicles, and perhaps a couple of dozen people by private train. The probable method of travel was to have the cars in baggage or box cars and the people in a Pullman car. These cars would be hooked to regularly scheduled trains and then dropped off on sidings at towns where the races were held. Rail service was much more extensive than it is now so this would work in most locations.

Private trains were not impossible—but do we believe J. Alex Sloan publicity or modern logic?

Transporters

Getting the race car to the track is a problem that has faced racers from day one. No need to go into how present-day racers do it—their fancy eighteen wheeler transporters cost more than most of us spent on the race cars in a career.

The first race cars were no doubt driven to the track, or maybe towed by a horse, but it didn't take long for race car owners to realize something better was needed. The 1920s and '30s racers came up with some interesting transportation devices. Happily, they took some photos of their creations.

Top: John Gerber started out with a pretty basic means of getting his bobtail to the race track. This is early in Gerber's career and the tow car is a 1922 Essex (Marty Brightman collection). *Bottom:* It can't get any simpler than this. San Jose, California, in 1927 (Jim Chini collection).

Top: L.M. Zirtzman used this trailer to get his #16 to a race at Garretson, South Dakota, in 1931. The axles of the race car rest directly on the trailer rails. It must have taken a bit of muscle to load and unload but the Model T's were light. *Bottom:* This is pretty much a typical trailer of the 1930s. The narrow roads of the era precluded building a wider trailer but on this rig the race car sits low. Someplace in South Dakota in 1932 (Both photographs—Wood collection).

Top: Bayliss Levrett built this rig to get his car from the San Francisco area to a 1936 race in Portland. The photograph was taken near the summit of the 6,000-foot Siskiyou Mountains. Going uphill was no doubt slow going for the Model A tow car—with those brakes it is scary to think about downhill! (Levrett collection). *Bottom:* Sig Haugdahl used this neat setup to haul his cars to a 1934 race at Davenport, Iowa. Both of the cars are Miller Eights (Jim Haag collection).

Top: Very few racers had pickups to tow with so the passenger car had to do. This was true until at least the 1960s (Bob Silvia collection). *Bottom:* Rajo Jack used this truck to haul his Miller from his Los Angeles home to race in Victoria, British Columbia. Here he is shown on the way home at Portland Speedway (Herman Giles collection).

14. The Way It Was 301

Top: Here is how the well financed owners did it in 1935. Gil Pirrung ran his car in several 1930s Indy races and probably used this same truck to haul it. This is the dirt car at an unknown track (Don Radbruch collection; photograph by Stewart). *Bottom:* Not an eighteen-wheeler, but nonetheless a long truck (Don Radbruch collection; photograph by Stewart).

Mystery Heads

During the 1920s and '30s dozens of manufacturers produced overhead valve heads for the Ford Model T and Model A-B engines, but OHV units for the flathead Ford V-8 were very rare. George Riley introduced an OHV unit in about 1937, and although it was reliable and produced good horsepower readings, it never really caught on. There were also Alexander OHV heads produced and maybe a few more makes that have been forgotten. A 1938 photograph of a southern California big car showed OHV heads that were different from any known prewar units.

The story of these heads is pieced together from a number of sources and may or may not be totally accurate. These four intake-four exhaust port heads were either

Left: The Dixon or Glendale OHV heads on a Ford V-8 in 1938. The photograph was probably taken at Southern Ascot Speedway in South Gate, California. The shape of the rocker arm covers and the location of the studs are different from the better-known units for the flathead V-8 (Johnny Klann collection). *Bottom:* Del Fanning's big car at Portland in 1947. The OHV heads are obviously similar to those on the 1938 California car. On paper the four-port head design sounds great, but for some reason they did not perform too well on the race track (Jack Greiner collection).

Dixon or Glendale heads. Some say they were built in southern California—this ties in nicely with Glendale. Other sources report that the heads were manufactured in the Pacific Northwest for use by the Dixon Lumber Company. (History shows that there was a Dixon Lumber Company in Portland, Oregon.) It seems that the Dixon Lumber Company wanted more power for their Ford V-8 lumber trucks and hoped to solve the constant overheating problem. Assuming the Dixon Lumber Company went ahead with its V-8 improvement project, it could be that they had the heads manufactured in the Los Angeles area and thus the confusion with the Glendale name. It also could be that Dixon had the heads built in the Pacific Northwest. A logical man for this job would be Glen Shaw in Seattle who built lots of racing parts for both the big cars and midgets. Just suppose *Glen* Shaw worked with somebody name "*Dale*"—yep, there's the other name tagged on to the mystery heads. It would be nice to say that extensive research confirmed this theory but this is not so—extensive research turned up nothing.

The Pacific Northwest connection was strengthened by racer Del Fanning of Seattle who used these heads on his big car in the late 1940s. Dixon, Glendale, or whatever, the heads might have been great on a lumber truck, but they were not very successful on Del Fanning's race car.

Ads and Programs

Early film star Wallace Reid made several racing movies. This 1922 advertisement appeared in a Vancouver, British Columbia, newspaper (Brian Pratt collection).

Old ads and racing programs are often as interesting as old race car photos. Here are a few that were collected during research for this book.

Pleasanton is about 30 miles east of Oakland in central California. Not many races were held here (Chick Lasteri collection).

Famous "Fronty" Dirt Track Winner

HERE'S the latest edition of the little speed devil that has copped more prizes and set more world's records than any other car in its class for years, and it has led more drivers into the big-time classics than any other — many drivers who have been world famous for years past. This car has made a record of 24 2/5 seconds for a half-mile dirt track at Jungle Park Speedway, Rockville, Ind. When it comes to "Fronty" racers or special racing cars, come to Arthur Chevrolet—the best and longest known designer, builder and driver of race cars in the business. His shop is also headquarters for special speed equipment for Fords, Chevrolets, Whippets — including cylinder heads, crank shafts, pistons, etc. We also make Frontenac cylinder heads for Ford and Chevrolet passenger cars which double their power and pick-up.

Call or write for catalog and prices

ARTHUR CHEVROLET AVIATION MOTORS CORP.

410 WEST TENTH ST.   (Formerly Chevrolet Bros. Mfg. Co.)   INDIANAPOLIS, IND.

For speed, power, silent operation. No regrinding. Save this cost in one ordinary valve grinding period.

BOYLE VALVE COMPANY
5821-3-5 South Ada Street

Top: Art Chevrolet would sell you a ready to go race car in 1928 (Murawaski collection). *Bottom:* The Boyle Valve Company used racing to promote their product in 1932 (Richard Andre collection).

Auto Races Sunday, Apr. 14
San Jose Speedway

Guaranteed Purse

$500

Plus 25% of Gate Over $2500

MAIN EVENT 50 LAPS

ONE MAN JOBS WANTED
Overhead cams allowed, depending on specifications.
Send pictures with entry. Entries Close April 7t

Write G. H. Gallineau, 652 Polk St., San Francisco

AAA RACE
ON
New ½-Mile Flat Track
Sunday MAY 26th
Oakland Speedway

$25.00 will be paid to each of the twelve fastest cars to qualify, brought from Los Angeles, in case they fail to win that amount.

SEND ENTRIES TO

OAKLAND SPEEDWAY, Inc.
E. L. MATHEWSON, Mgr.

Leamington Hotel   Oakland, Calif.

Top left: This ad was in a 1935 issue of *Coast Auto Racing*. Not a bad purse—probably about $100 to win the main. *Top right:* Another *Coast Auto Racing* ad. Oakland was dependent on Los Angeles cars to have an adequate field—hence the reasonably generous guarantee offer. *Bottom:* This 1935 *Coast Auto Racing* ad is for a race on Oakland's mile track—this would be the last year the AAA ran at Oakland. An ad like this probably cost in the neighborhood of five dollars (All photographs—Don Radbruch collection).

100-LAP RACE
ON MILE TRACK
Sunday, June 23rd
AT
Oakland, Calif.

WITH LEADING A.A.A. DRIVERS

100-MILE MAIN EVENT—10-MILE HEATS AND
10-MILE CLASS B RACE

Right: Lee Chapel wanted to move his operation to the San Francisco area and ran this ad in *Coast Auto Racing*. If he wound up trading for a battleship he must have made millions re-selling it to the United States Navy a few years later when World War II broke out (Don Radbruch collection). *Bottom:* This is from a flier mailed to racers all over the country. Was this a workshop-type thing, or one hell of a party? (Gemsa collection from Marty Brightman).

Top: Promoters advertised heavily in national racing publications. This one was in *Illustrated Speedway News* in 1939 (Don Radbruch collection). *Bottom:* This *Illustrated Speedway News* ad from 1939 boasts of "reduced prices." It sounds cheap but remember times have changed.

MOVIE STARS TURN DAREDEVILS Pat O'Brien and Frank McHugh movie stars (above) give a credible performance as race car speedsters in the picture "Indianapolis Speedway". This thriller will be shown at the Strand Theatre N. Y. week of July 14th.

Movie promos made their way into racing newspapers—*Illustrated Speedway News* in 1939. *Indianapolis Speedway* was a rather poor remake of the epic, *The Crowd Roars!* Much of the same racing footage was used and poor old Frank McHugh gets killed again (Don Radbruch collection).

The Crowd Roars

There were a couple of dozen racing movies made in the 1920s and 1930s. Most were thoroughly forgettable from both artistic and racing viewpoints.

The best of the lot was the 1932 Warner Brothers film, *The Crowd Roars*, starring James Cagney. As youngsters, some of us saw the classic and it can still be enjoyed on late-night-TV old movies. The plot is best ignored but there are some good racing scenes. Early in the film Cagney and his buddy, Frank McHugh, are racing on a dusty dirt oval—these scenes were shot at the Pomona Fairgrounds in Southern California. Then it is on to Legion Ascot for some good night racing action. (Frank McHugh dies in a very phony crash.) Indy is next with the two-man cars. Oh how Hollywood loved these machines! The two characters could shout at each other in a very dramatic manner. It is a bit surprising that Hollywood isn't still running the two-man cars at Indy under the assumption that nobody would know the difference.

The Crowd Roars was not one of Cagney's greatest hits. The film got terrible reviews—the following is quoted from the *New York Times*: "Mr. Cagney delivers as much force in his role as is possible. Joan Blondell and Ann Dvorak also serve their parts capably, but there is nothing edifying in their lines. The outstanding sequences in this film are those depicting the various automobile races, but even then, one's eardrums are sorely tired."

Aw, come on, Mr. Reviewer, the roar of the race cars was the best part!

Index

Numbers in **boldface** indicate photographs.

Abbott, Charles **196**
Aberdeen SD 98, 113
Abilene TX **89**, 92, 94, 127, 155
Ada MN **105**
Adair, Les **174**
Adams, Babe 81
Adams, Howard "Speed" **142**
Agabashian, Fred 42, **43**, 277
Agabashian, Mabel **26**
Agajanian, J.C. 42, **46**, 48
Akron OH 178
Alabama State Fairgrounds 242; see also Birmingham AL
Alan Track ID see Post Falls ID
Albany GA 250
Alberts, Pete (aka Pietro Alberti) **174**
Albuquerque NM, All American Speedway, Hells Half Acre Speedway 89, **94**
Alden, Frank **190**
Alder, Walt **226**
Aledo IL **140**
All American Speedway NM see Albuquerque NM
Allen, Ed **260**
Allentown Fairgrounds PA 215, 228
Allentown PA 202
Alridge, Doc **101**
Altamont NY 192
The Alternate v, 3
Altoona Board Track PA 215
Altoona Fairgrounds PA 215
Ambler Brothers 220, 221
American Automobile Association (AAA) 6, 7, 9, 12, 15, 18, 25, 27, 43, 44, 47, 53, 54, 56, 62, 63, 68, 71, 72, 77, 82, 84, 86, 88, 92, 94, 98, 108, 115, 133, 135, 139, 154, 155, 156, 164, 167, 169, 171, 172, 173, 174, 187, 189, 193, 202, 211, 213, 219, 222, 235, 241, 243, 248, 249, 251,
254, 259, 266, 267, 277, 291, 306
American Racing Association (ARA) 3, 42, 47, 154
American Racing Drivers Club (ARDC) 202
Andalusia AL 242
Anderson, Andy 74
Anderson, Les **39**
Andres, Emil **146, 147,** 168
Angell Park Speedway WI see Sun Prairie WI
Angeloni, Harry 237
Ann Arbor MI 159
Anthony KS 113, **121**, 130
Arden Downs PA see Washington PA
Ardmore OK 116, 122
Arkansas City KS 113
Arkansas State Fairgrounds see Little Rock AR 242
Arlington TX see Fort Worth TX
Arnold, Billy **23**, 157
Arnz, Tex **230**
Arrowhead Park Speedway see Houston TX
Ashland KY 241
Ashley PA 229
Athol MA 193
Atlanta GA, Atlanta Motordrome, Atlanta Speedway, Hamilton Speedway 249
Atlanta GA, Lakewood Speedway 249, **252**
Auburn 214
Augustine Beach Speedway DE see Fort Penn DE
Aurora Downs IL see Chicago IL
Aurora Speedway (Speedbowl) WA see Seattle WA
Austin MN 98
Austin TX 92, 97
Auto Racing Association (ARA) 236, 237
Auto Racing Memories 3, 252
Automobile Quarterly 203
Avon CT 193
Axel, Lloyd 7, **72, 73, 74, 137,** 138

Bagley, John **113**, 133, 135, 142
Bagley, Sam **115**
Baker (Baker City) OR 87
Baker, Clyde and Alma 133
Bakersfield CA (Derkum Dirt Track) 12
Bakersfield CA, Kern County Fairgrounds, Derkum Dirt Track 12
Bales, Red **175**
Balmer, Everett 7
Baltimore MD **216**
Baltimore MD, Electric Park, Pimlico Horse Track, Gentlemen's Driving Park 218
Banks, Henry **186**
Banning CA 14, **18, 19, 20, 21**
Barber, Dick 37
Barbo, Chick **66**
Barnett, Ed 49
Barnett, Waldo **117, 118, 119**
Baton Rouge LA 243
Bay Cities Racing Association (BCRA) 3, 43, 194
Bay Meadows CA **202**
Beardsly, Bill **103**
Beatrice NE **126**
Beaumont TX 92, 122
Beaver Dam WI 139
Beckett, Larry **252**
Becktloff, Bob 237
Bedford IA 139
Bedford PA 229
Bedford Park CT see New Haven CT
Bel Aire MD 218

311

Index

Bellaire Track TX *see* Houston TX
Belleville KS 102, 111, 113, **120**, 127, 130, 133
Belmont PA *see* Philadelphia PA
Bemidji MN 98
Bend OR 11
Bennettsville SC 249
Benning Speedway DC *see* Washington DC
Bennington VT, Burgess Field 189
Bentley **213**, 214
Bergen Herald 278
Bertrand, Pierre **44**
Bettenhausen, Tony 47
Beulah Park OH *see* Columbus OH
Beverly Hills CA, Board Track 14
Bianchi, Mario **32**, 60, 77, 78, **261**, 266
Billings MT 68
Billman, Mike **136**
Biltmore Hotel, Dayton OH 307
Bingingham NY 192
Bird-in-Hand PA, Central Speedway 194, 215, **229**, **231**, 233
Birmingham AL, Alabama State Fairgrounds 242, 288
Bisbee AZ (Bisbee Trophy) **95**, 96
Bismarck ND 98
Black Demon Speedway IN *see* Terre Haute IN
Bland, Eddie 252
Blondell, Joan 310
Bloom, Tip 266
Bloomgren, Bert **265**
Blytheville AR 242
Bo Sterns Track KS *see* Wichita KS
Bob, Joe **194**
Boise ID 68, 87
Bonneville Salt Flats UT **78**
Booker, Elbert "Pappy" **171**
Bowan 122
Boyer, Lillian 288
Boyle Valve Company **305**
Branchero, Mario **26**, **40**
Brandon, Manitoba (Canada) 259
Branton, Bob **270**
Bray, Rea **49**
Bray Brook Oval NY *see* Staten Island NY
Breckenridge Speedway, Alberta (Canada) *see* Edmonton
Breckenridge TX 92, **93**
Breshauer, Ken 3
Brightman, Marty 53
Brighton Beach NY *see* Brooklyn NY
Brisco, Frank **166**
Bristol CT 193
British Columbia Automotive Sports Association (BCASA) 266

Brockton MA, Brockton Fairgrounds 193, **195**, **197**, 208, **209**
Brooklyn MD 218
Brooklyn NY, Brighton Beach, Sheepshead Bay 192
Brookpark, Cleveland OH 162
Brown, Allan v, 159, 256
Brown, Babe *see* Adair, Les
Brown, Walt **237**
Brunk, Earl 73
Brunots Island PA *see* Pittsburgh PA
Brunswick ME, Topsham Fairgrounds 189
Bryan, Bobby **89**
Buffalo NY 192
Bullock, Noel 71, 81, **82**, **112**, 127
Bumpus, Howard "Bumpy" **200**
Burd Piston Ring Special **224**
Burgess Field VT *see* Bennington VT
Burkitt, Neeley 37, 65
Burlington IA 139
Burlington IN 161
Burman, Bob 211, **212**
Burnaugh, Cecil **120**
Burnett, Dud 81
Burton, Clyde 156, 157
Byberry PA *see* Philadelphia PA

Cabarrus District Fairgrounds NC *see* Concord NC 248
Cadillac MI 159
Cagney, James 309
Caldwell, R.W. **129**
Caledonia NY 192
Calgary, Alberta (Canada), Calgary Industrial Exhibition 257
California Dirt Track Kings 266
Calistoga CA 12
Callaway, Buddy **150**, **169**, **251**
Calumet IL *see* Chicago IL
Cambridge MA, Charles River Park 192
Cambridge MD 218
Camden NJ 218
Camp Foster FL **252**
Camp Foster TN *see* Chattanooga TN 241
Campbell, Peaches 132
Campbell, Red 142
Canadian National Expo *see* Toronto
Canapwa, George **195**
Canino, Jimmy **200**
Canobie Lake NH 189
Cantlon, Shorty **149**, **165**, 290
Canton OH 162
Cape Girardeau MO 144, 173
Carey, Bob 184, 187, **286**
Carmody, Jack 26, 277
Carter, Duane **26**, **40**, 228
Carthage MO 144
Casa Grande AZ 89

Cassiday, Wild Bill **220**
Cedar Rapids IA 133, 139, **146**, **148**
Cedarburg WI 139
Central Pennsy Racing Association 229, 230, 232, 233, 234, 236
Central Speedway PA *see* Bird-in-Hand PA
Central States Racing Association (CSRA) 6, 105, 131, 143, 145, 173, 176, 180 187 195
Centralia WA 10
Challenger, Art **108**
Chamberlain, Ted 235, **236**
Champeau, Dave **105**
Chapel, Lee (Lee's Speed Shop) 307
Charles River Park MA *see* Cambridge MA
Charlotte NC, Southern States Fairgrounds 248
Charter Oaks Park MA *see* Hartford MA
Chatham, Ontario (Canada) 259
Chattanooga TN, Camp Foster, Warner Park 241
Chevrolet, Arthur 6, 165, 305
Chevrolet, Gaston 235
Chicago IL, Aurora Downs, Calumet, Hawthorne, North Shore 141
Chicago IL, Sparta Stadium 143
Chico CA 151
Childress TX **88**, 92, 122
Chitum, Bill 185
Chitwood, Joie **90**, 131, 138, **175**, **227**, **234**, **237**
Chowchilla CA 12, 53
Churchill, Phil 266
Cincinnati OH, Cincinnati-Hamilton Speedway, Hamilton Fairgrounds 162
Clancy, Paul 81
Clarion PA 215
Clark, Henry 291, 292
Clark, J.D. 83
Clark, Maynard "Hungry" **115**, 145
Clark, Sim **194**, 195
Clarksburg WV 221, **280**
Clearfield PA 215, 229
Cleveland OH, Glenville Driving Park, Brookpark, Randall Park, Thistledowns 161, 162
Cocoa Beach FL 251
Cohokia IL 150
Cole, Hal 7, 46, **48**, 172
Collins, Emory **100**, **116**, 132, 138, **145**, **258**, 292, 293
Collins, Myke 210, **211**
Colorado Springs CO 71
Columbia SC 249
Columbus OH, Columbus Driving Park, Beulah Park 162

Index

Columbus OH, Ohio State Fairgrounds 162, **244**
Colwood Park, British Columbia (Canada) *see* Victoria, British Columbia
Concord NC, Cabarrus District Fairgrounds 248
Connally, "One Eye" **204**
Cook County Fairgrounds 143, **150, 151**
Corbitt, Clay 185
Corpus Christi TX 97
Costa, Jimmy 81, 251
Cotter, Clair **107**
Council Grove KS 113
Courtney, Ray 172, **173**
Covington County Fairgrounds AL *see* Andalusia AL 243
Covington KY 241
Covington LA 243
Cox, Howard **28**
Cranston RI, Narragansett Park 194, 211, **212, 213**, 213
Criss, Ernie 39
Crossbay Speedway *see* New York City NY, Queens
The Crowd Roars 309, 310
Crown Point IN 161
Culp, Dutch 229
Culver City Board Track CA 17
Culver City CA 14, **15, 50, 51**
Cummings, Bill **287**, 290
Cunningham, Pat **61**, 79, 94, **116**, 129, 130, **136, 276, 277**
Curryer, Charlie 46, 47, **48**
Curtis, Frank 237
Cushing OK 116
Cutter, Bob 229

Dallas TX 89, 97
Dallas TX, Cotton Bowl, Industrial, Love Field, Walnut Hill 92
Danbury CT, Danbury Fair 193, **196**
Dans, Adolph 37
Darlington SC 211
Davenport IA, Mississippi Valley Fairgrounds 139, **299**
Davis, Floyd 224, **227**
Davis, Sam **161**
Davis, Ted 118
Davis, Walt **40**
Dawson MI 159
Dayton OH, Dayton Speedway **130**, 162, **171**, 176
Dayton OH, Montgomery County Fairgrounds 162
Daytona Beach FL, Daytona Beach Speedway 163, 245, 248, 249, 250, 253, 254
DeBell, Leonard 65
Deer Park NY 192
DeFrates, Pont 148

DeLand FL, DeLand Fairgrounds **250, 251**
Delaware State Fairgrounds *see* Harrington DE
Del Mar CA 54, 172
Delphos KS 113
Delvenux, Leon 81
Denver CO, Merchants Park **75, 76**
Denver CO, Overland Park, 68, 69, **70, 71, 72**, 84, 85, 127, 133, 288
DePalma, Ralph **15, 56, 57, 58**, 71, 143, 210, 211, 249
DePaulo, Peter 92
Derkum Dirt Track CA *see* Bakersfield CA
De Schanck, Felix 81
Deshler NE 113
Deslormiers Park, Quebec (Canada) *see* Montreal, Quebec
Des Moines IA 139, **153**
Detroit MI, Michigan State Fairgrounds 158, **165, 166, 167, 168**
Detroit MI, V.F.W. Speedway (aka Motor City Speedway) 158, 184, **185, 186, 187**
Devine, Phyllis v, 3
Devore, Earl 71
Dewey OK 116
Dighton KS 113
Dinsmore, Duke 76, **137**, 138
Dixie Speedway VA *see* Norfolk VA
Dodge City KS 113
Dolan, "One Lap" **207**
Dothan AL 243
Douglas AZ 83, **95**, 96
Dover NH, Granite Park Speedway 189, **191**, 206
Downing, Sharon 74
Dreselhuys, Fred **102**
Drexler, Shorty **169, 197**
DuBois PA, Gateway Fairgrounds 215
Dudley, Ray 61
Duncan OK 92, 94
Duncan, Len **237, 239**
Duncan, Les **178**
Dunkirk NY 192
Dunlop, Andy **200**
Dupont CO **70**, 71, 75, 80
DuQuoin IL 141
Durant Louis 7, 274
Duray, Gus 78, 266
Duray, Leon (aka George Stewart) 71, 178
Dusang, Roy **257**
Dusselheys, Fred **115**
Dvorak, Ann 310

Earl, Murray **116, 118**
Earle, Jack 117
East Lansing MI 159

Eastern Museum of Motor Racing 181
Eastern States Expo Speedway MA *see* West Springfield MA
Eaton, Roy 153, 154
Ebersole, Ebby **230**
Economaki, Chris 215, **228**, 280
Edmonton, Alberta (Canada), Breckenridge Speedway 259
Electric Park MD *see* Baltimore MD
Elkins WV 221
Elma WA 11
El Paso TX 92, 97
Epson Downs TX *see* Houston TX
Escanaba MI 159
Eslmere Fairgrounds DE 221
Essex Junction VT 189, 308
Essex, Ontario (Canada) 259
Evans, Pop 9, 22, 23, 26, 48, 50, **90, 91**
Evanston IL **147**
Everett WA, Silverlake (Silver Lake) Speedway 35

Fairmont MN 98
Fairmount Park PA *see* Philadelphia PA
Fanning, Del **302**, 303
Fargo ND 98
Farmer, Don **64**
Farmington NJ 86
Favinger, John **231**
Fayetteville AR 242
Felt, Vic 72, 74, 76, **137**, 138
Fenno, Lew **115**
Ficken, Bert **115, 136**
Fiore, Mike **192**
Fisher, Burt 138
Flagstaff AZ **91**
Flemington NJ 200, **204**, 215, 228, 308
Florida State Fairgrounds *see* Tampa FL
Foanpaugh, Ernie 91
Fonda NY 192
Ford, Henry 158
Forestburg SD, Ruskin Track **100**, 101
Fort Erie, Ontario (Canada) 259
Fort Miami Speedway, OH *see* Toledo OH
Fort Penn DE, Augustine Beach Speedway 211
Fort Wayne IN, Fort Wayne Driving Park 159
Fort Wayne IN, Fort Wayne Speedway **170**, 176
Fort William, Ontario (Canada) 259
Fort Worth TX, Arlington 92
Foster, Phil 260, **261**, 266, 271, 272
Fowler, Ken **221**

Fowlerville MI 159
Foyt, A.J. 92, **228**
Frame, Fred **92**, **93**, 94, **154**, **155**, **156**, 223, 290
Franazo, Campie **186**
France, Bill 249, **252**
Frank, Vern 186, **187**
Franklin IN 174
Franklin NE, Senter Park **111**, 113, **128**
Fred Buckmiller Track SD *see* Sioux Falls SD
Frederick OK 122
Fredrick MD 218
Freehold NJ 218
Freeman, Curley **115**
Freeman, Joe 203
French, Harley **206**
Fresno CA 12
Fromm, Paul **22**, 54
Fuller, Andrew 138
Fulton KY 241
Funk, Frank **282**

Galveston TX 89
Garden States Racing Association (GSRA) 237
Gardina, Tony 210
Gardner, Augusta 83, 86
Gardner, Buster 88
Gardner, Chet 71, **84**, **85**, **89**, 92, 94, **95**, 146, **284**, 290
Gardner, Dean 83, 84
Gardner, Fay 114, **115**
Gardner, Howard 72, 83, 86, 94
Gardner, Jack 83
Gardner, Jack, Jr. 83
Gardner, James D. 83
Gardner, Jeff 83
Gardner, Jimmy 83
Gardner, Ray **70**, 72, **84**, **85**, **92**, **95**
Gardner, Red 86, 87
Garretson SD **298**
Garrett, Tom **112**
Gast, Ray **249**, **250**, **251**
Gast, Ray, Mrs. **250**
Gasta, Al **229**, **231**
Gateway Fairgrounds PA *see* DuBois PA
Gayden, Ernest **140**
Gentlemen's Driving Park MD *see* Baltimore MD
Gentry, Harry **24**
Gerber, John 120, 122, 124, 135, **136**, **143**, 145, 150, 230, **297**
Gernere, Don **226**
Gessell, Ernie **201**, **210**, **222**
Gettysburg SD **109**
Gilbert, Clyde "Tiny" **75**, **118**, **136**, **137**, 138
Giles, Herman 53
Gilmore Stadium CA *see* Los Angeles CA
Giroux, Ben *see* Gotoff, Ben
Giullano, Louie **200**

Glenville Driving Park, Cleveland OH 161
Golden Submarine 159
Golden Wheels 3
Goodland KS 113
Gordon, Al 47
Goshen CA 12, **44**
Gotoff, Ben (aka Ben Giroux) 69, 80, **158**, 176, **177**, **242**
Grable, Cotton **251**
Grand Forks ND 98
Grand Rapids MI 158
Granite State Park Speedway *see* Dover NH
Grant Park WI *see* Milwaukee WI
Grants Pass OR 11
Great Bend KS 127
Great Falls MT 68
Greely CO **74**
Green, Bob **252**
Green, Leigh **15**
Greensboro NC 248
Greenville OH 173
Gresham Speedbowl OR *see* Portland OR
Grim, Bobby 143
Groesbeck TX 92, 122
Groose Point MI 158
Grossbeck TX 122
Guisti, Adolph **16**, 58
Gulf Coast TX *see* Houston TX
Guttenburg NJ 215

Haddad, Ed 7
Hagerstown MD 218
Haibe, Ora 216
Halifax, Nova Scotia (Canada), Halifax Exhibition Track 260
Hamilton Fairgrounds OH *see* Cincinnati OH
Hamilton Speedway GA *see* Atlanta GA
Hammond IN 161; *see also* Roby Speedway
Hammond IN, Hammond Speedway 161, **178**, **179**, **180**, **281**
Hankinson, Ralph 156, 234, 259, **280**
Hannahan Farm NH *see* West Swanzey NH
Hansen, Mel **266**, 277
Harding, Bill **119**
Hardy, "Cowboy" **146**
Harlingen TX 92, 122
Harrington DE, Kent-Sussex County Fairgrounds (Delaware State Fairgrounds) 218
Harris, Pete **206**
Harroun, Ray 241, 249
Hart, Harry **75**, **120**
Hartford CT, Charter Oaks Park 193
Hartford KY 241

Harton, Earl **175**
Harton, Zook 173
Hartz, Harry 71
Haskell TX 90
Haskill, Clarence **136**
Hastings NE 113
Hastings Park, British Columbia (Canada) *see* Vancouver B.C.
Hatfield PA 215
Hatton and Hurst Circuit 122
Haugdahl, Sig 71, **105**, 177, 253, 254, **255**, **299**
Haupt, Willy 211
Hawkes, Douglas W. 214
Hawthorne IL *see* Chicago IL
Hearne, Eddie 44, 56, **57**, **58**
Heber, Art **232**
Hebert, Ray **104**, **157**
Helena MT **69**
Hells Half Acre Speedway NM *see* Albuquerque NM
Hemmingway, Ernest 55
Henry, Hank 292
Hepburn, Ralph 159
Hershey PA **182**, **234**
Hibbing MN 98
Hill, Ernie 133
Hiller (Hillier), Robert 266
Himes, Bill 133
Hinkley, Speed **18**
Hinnershitz, Tommy **229**, 234
Hipnett, Herb **19**
History of America's Speedways v, 159, 256
Hobart OK 116, 122
Hodges, Red **91**
Hoffman, Sam **74**, **104**, 130, 135, **136**, **142**, **144**, **148**
Hoft, Joe
Ho-Ho-Kus NJ 215, **222**, **228**
Holden, Tom **120**
Holdrege NE **112**
Holland, Bill **239**
Hollbrook, Merle 74
Holmes, Bill **237**
Holmes, Jackie **195**
Holmes Airport Speedway *see* New York City, NY
Hood, Frank 284
Hooker, Harry 21
Hooker Model T **21**
Hopp, Al 266
Horey, Fred **158**, 177, 243, **244**, 245, 246, 266
Horn, Ted 54, 65, **226**, **234**, **237**
Horner, Billy 235
Houck, Monte **11**
Householder, Ronnie **150**
Houston, Fred 130
Houston TX, Bellaire Track, Epson Downs, Gulf Coast, South Main, Arrowhead Park Speedway 92
Hughes, Ed 122

Index

Hughes, Lawrence 122, **123, 125, 126**
Hughes Stadium CA *see* Sacramento CA
Huntington Speedway CT *see* Sheldon CT
Huntington VT 189
Huntsville AL, Madison County Fairgrounds 243
Huron SD, State Fair Speedway 98
Hutchinson KS 113, **117**

Ianacone, Gus 237
Iddings, John 182
Iddings Special 182
Illustrated Speedway News 3, 252, 309
Independence MO 144
Indiana PA 215
Indianapolis IN, Indiana State Fairgrounds 159
Indianapolis Speedway 309
Indianapolis Speedway (Indy) 43, 44, 47, 53, 54, 56, 57, 62, 63, 85, 92, 94, 98, 104, 108, 145, 148, 150, 154, 155, 159, 165, 166, 167, 169, 171, 173, 174, 175, 182, 184, 199, 202, 211
Ingleside Track CA *see* San Francisco CA
Insinger, Harris **286**
International Motor Contest Association (IMCA) 6, 44, 52, 53, 67, 68, 71, 79, 84, 85, 98, 105, 107, 113, 115, 131, 143, 145, 158, 159, 163, 169, 177, 189, 193, 197
Interstate Fairgrounds IA *see* Sioux City IA
Inter-State Fairgrounds NJ *see* Trenton NJ
Interstate Fairgrounds WA *see* Spokane WA
Ionia MI **289**
Iron Mountain MI 159

Jack, Rajo **11, 12, 28, 48, 49, 50, 51, 52, 53, 63, 153, 300**
Jack, Ruth or Estelle **50**
Jackson MI 158
Jackson MS, Mississippi State Fairgrounds 243
Jacksonville FL 250, 251, 288
Jacobs, Max 292
Jarvie, Floyd **224**
Jefferson City MO 144
Jenkens, Ab 79
Jenkins, Hick **250**
Jennerstown PA 215
Jennings, Windy **172, 176**
Johnson, Bill **41, 48**
Johnson City TN 241
Johnstown PA, Luna Park 235
Johnstown Tribune 235

Joliet IL 292
Jones, Grace 245
Jones, Warren 53
Jonesboro AR 241
Jungle Park IN 159, **173**

Kalamazoo MI 155, 158
Kansas City MO **132**, 143
Karnatz, Burt **167**
Karp, Al **161**
Kearny NE 113
Keene NH 189, **193, 196, 199**
Kelchner, Armon 229, **230, 240**
Kenealy, Mel **21, 30, 32, 294**
Kennebunk ME 189
Kennedy, Captain 80, 81
Kent-Suffix County Fairgrounds DE *see* Harrington DE
Kentucky Motor Speedway *see* Louisville KY
Kentucky State Fairgrounds *see* Louisville KY
Kerbs, Leonard 7, 114, **127**, 129, 130, 133, 135
Kern County Fairgrounds CA *see* Bakersfield CA
Killinger, Walt **75**
Kimball SD 98
King, Bob **191**
Kinser, Steve 101, 182
Kinston Fairgrounds NC 248
Klamath Falls OR 11
Klann, Johnny 18, **22**, 44, **45**
Klaupher, Barney 25
Kleinau, Lou 2
Knight, Jimmy **237**
Knoxville IA 139
Koetzla, Dave **177, 257**
Kraft, George **100**
Krasek, Leo **146,** 151
Krieger, Johnny 138
Kurtis, Frank 65
Kutztown PA 215

LaCosta, Joan 288
Lafayette IN 161
Lagoon UT *see* Salt Lake City UT
Laguna Seca CA 3
Laird, Jimmy **269**
Lake City FL 251
Lakeville MA 193
Lakewood Speedway GA *see* Atlanta GA
Landisville PA 229
Langford Speedway, British Columbia (Canada) *see* Victoria B.C.
Langhorne Speedway PA 47, 105, **154**, 215, **223**, **224**, **225**, 228, 236
Lapp, George **260**
La Rosa, Bill 53
Larson, Emmet **19**

Larson, Kenny "Cementhead" 109, 110
Lastiri, Chick 49
Laterimore Valley Fairgrounds PA **182**
Laurel MD 71
Laurel MS 243
Laureldale MD 218
Lavelle, Jack **196**
Lawrence KS 113
Lawton OK 116
Leamington, Ontario (Canada) 259, **283**
Lebanon KY 241
Lebanon PA 229, 230, **231**, 232, **236**
Lecero, John 44
Lee, Stan 110
Legge, Tommy **176**
Legion Ascot Speedway 44
Legion Ascot Speedway CA *see* Los Angeles CA
Lehighton PA 229
Letcher SD 98
Levrett, Bayliss **27, 28**, 63, **180, 181, 195, 251, 299**
Lewis, Ace **193**
Lewis, Lew 284
Lewiston ME 189
Lexington KY 241
Light, Mark 229, 230, **231**, 232
Lincoln NE 113
Lindskog, Swede **30, 265, 270, 277**
Lipscomb, Bill **62**
Little, Mike **238**
Little Rock AR, Arkansas State Fairgrounds 242
Livingston MT 68
Logan, Christine Horey 245
Long Island NY 189, 221
Los Angeles CA, Agricultural Park, Mines Field 14
Los Angeles CA, Ascot Park 10, 14, **16**, 44
Los Angeles CA, Gilmore Stadium 63, 91, 257
Los Angeles CA, Legion Ascot Speedway 7, 9, 14, 15, 38, 43, 54, 60, 65, 79, 86 145, 149, 164, 168, 223
Los Angeles CA, Southern Ascot Speedway *see* South Gate CA
Los Banos CA **10**, 12
Lott, George 266
Louisiana State Fairgrounds *see* Shreveport LA
Louisville KY, Kentucky State Fairgrounds, Kentucky Motor Speedway 241
Lucke, E.J. **18**
Luelling, Fred **16, 18**

MacKenzie, Doc **167, 227**
Macon GA **249,** 250

Index

Madison County Fairgrounds AL *see* Huntsville AL
Mahony, Stan 38
Mais, Elfrieda 288, **289**, **290**
Manchester NH 206
Mankato MN 98
Manley, George **199**
Mansell, Earl 7, **29**, **91**, 129, **291**, 292
Mardi Gras Track LA *see* New Orleans LA
Mario, Fat **26**, **40**
Marion, Milt **149**
Marion OH 163
Marshfield MA 193
Martino, Nick 60
Martinson, Art 7, **79**, 80
Maspeth Fairgrounds *see* New York City NY, Queens
Mauro, Johnny **121**
Mays, Phil 196
Mays, Rex 22, 53, **54**, **55**, 172, 223, **225**, **287**
Mazon IL 202
McCombs, Vernon **163**
McDowell, Johnny **35**
McGee, Billy **172**
McGurk, Frank 7
McHugh, Frank **309**
McKee, Mel 79
McMillen, Harry 81
McMinnville OR 11
McMurtry, Lew **35**, **265**
McWorter, Howard **99**
Mechanicsburg PA, Williams Grove Speedway 234, **237**
Medford OR 11
Memphis TN 241
Mendenhall, Buzz 180
Merchants Park CO *see* Denver CO
Meridian MS, Mississippi-Alabama State Fairgrounds 243
Meridian Speedway KS *see* Wichita KS
Merzney, Fred **70**, 71
Meyer, Bob 182
Meyer, Henry 180, **181**, 182
Meyer, Lou 267, **286**, 290
Michigan State Fairgrounds MI *see* Detroit MI
Middletown NY 192, **193**, **199**
Midwest Whispers 182
Mikkelsen, Carl **17**
Milbank SD 98, 100, **101**
Milburn, Harry 94, 95
Miles City MT 68
Milford DE 221
Miller, Al 185
Miller, Chet **165**
Miller, Harry 5, 21
Mills, Curley **23**, **28**, 44, 90
Milos, Matt **36**
Milton, Tommy 253

Milwaukee WI, Grant Park, South Milwaukee Speedway 139
Milwaukee WI, Milwaukee Mile 139, **149**, **166**, **169**, **174**, **175**
Mineola, Long Island NY 202
Mineral Wells TX 89
Mines Field CA *see* Los Angeles CA
Minot ND, Kodak Speedway 98
Minyard, Bud 63
Mississippi-Alabama State Fairgrounds MS *see* Meridian MS and Tupelo MS
Mississippi State Fairgrounds *see* Jackson MS
Missoula MT 68, **80**
Mitchell, Bill **190**
Mobile AL 243
Monnmouth Fairgrounds NJ *see* Oceanport NJ
Montgomery County Fairgrounds OH *see* Dayton OH
Montreal, Quebec (Canada), Deslormiers Park 260
Moon, Jack 237
Moore, Bob 182
Moore, Lou 290
Moore, Wes **272**, 273
Moremore, Chet **91**
Morosco, Felix **142**, **144**
Moross, Ernie 78
Morris, Doc 214
Morris, Harry 104
Morris Park NY *see* New York City NY, Bronx
Morrisette, Everett **191**
Morrisville VT 189
Moscow-Odessa Road Race, Russia 177
Motor City Speedway MI *see* Detroit MI
Moundsville WV 221
Mt. Clemens MI 159, **182**, **183**, 184
Mt. Holly NJ 218
Mt. Vernon IL 174
Muir, Norman **45**
Mulfinger, Rudy **115**
Mundy, Les *see* Adair, Les
Murfreesboro TN 241
Murillo, Ontario (Canada) 259
Murphy, Jimmy 192, **294**, 214
Musick, Ben (Bill Morris) **131**, **137**
Musick, Cecil 130
Musick, Cotton 133
Musick, Elmer Ray (Rabbit) **132**
Musick, Leland **132**, 133
Musick, Lynton (Len) **131**, 132
Musick, Morris **130**, **137**
Muskogee OK 115

Nalon, Duke **237**

Narragansett Park (Narragansett Speedway) RI *see* Cranston RI
NASCAR 236
Nashville TN, Tennessee State Fairgrounds 142, 241
National Auto Racing Association (NARA) 236, 237
National Championship Drivers of America (NCDA) 290, 291
National Speed Sport News (National Auto Racing News) 182, 196, 210, 228, 234, 266, **276**, 277, 278, 279, 280
National Speed Sport News (National Auto Racing News) Foto Review **278**, **279**, 280
National Sprint Car Hall of Fame 53, 182
Neals Speedway CA *see* San Diego CA
Nebraska Hot Rod Racing Association 124
Neil's Sportsman Park CA *see* San Diego CA
Neligh NE 113, 114, **115**
New Bedford MA 193
New Braunfels TX 122
New Bremen OH 162, **181**, 184
New Castle DE 221
New Haven CT, Bedford Park 193
New Kensington PA 215
New Market NH 189, **190**
New Market NJ 204, **205**, 210, 218
New Orleans LA, Mardi Gras Track 243
New Ulm MN 98
New York City NY, Bronx, Morris Park 192
New York City NY, Manhattan 192
New York City NY, Queens, Crossbay Speedway 192, 210
New York City NY, Queens, Holmes Airport Speedway, Maspeth Fairgrounds 192
New York State Fairgrounds *see* Syracuse
New York Times 310
Newhall CA 12
Newman, Vic **240**
Newport Fairgrounds RI 194
Niday, Cal 135, 138
Nikrent, Joe 244
Noe, Pappy **91**
Norfolk Fairgrounds VA *see* Norfolk VA
Norfolk VA, Dixie Speedway, Norfolk Fairgrounds, Princess Anne 222
North Gloucester ME 189
North Shore IL *see* Chicago IL
Northampton MA 193
Northwest Dirt Track Drivers Association 100

Northwest Vintage Speedster Club 122
Norwalk OH, Huron County Fairgrounds 175
Norwich CT 193
Norwood, Ontario (Canada) 259
Nowles, Johnny 197
Nutley NJ, Nutley Stadium 221
Nyquist, Ted 229, **231**

Oakes, Danny 138
Oakland CA, Board Track 243
Oakland CA, Exposition Building 3
Oakland CA, Oakland Speedway 9, **23**, 24, 37, 39, **40**, **41**, 42, **43**, 45, 46, 47, 49, 53, **65**, **66**, 67, 83, 85, **156**, 274, **275**, **276**, 277, 284, 291, 306
Oakland Tribune 277
Oakley KS 113
O'Brian, Pat **309**
Oceanport NJ, Monnmouth Fairgrounds 215
O'Day, Offy **174**
Ohio State Fairgrounds *see* Columbus OH
Oklahoma City OK 111, **282**
Old Orchard Beach ME 187, **208**
Old Orchard ME 189
Oldfield, Barney 71, 159, **163**, 241, 249, 250
Olympic View Speedway WA *see* Seattle WA
Omaha NE 111
Onley, Mr. 122
Opelika AL 243
Orangeburg SC 249
Ord NE 81, 113, **126**, 133, **134**, **135**, **136**
Ord Quiz 133
Ormand Beach FL 250
Ormsby, Ralph, Jr. 278
O'Rourke, Cowboy **222**
Osark Empire Fair MO *see* Springfield MO
Oshkosh NE 113
Oshkosh WI 139
Osmer, Harold 187
Outlaw Sprint Car Racer 122
Overland Park CO *see* Denver CO

Painsville IL **172**
Palmer, Sam **303**
Parana, Argentina **283**
Parent, Ronnie **287**
Paris MO 154
Parkersburg WV 221
Pascoag RI 194
Patterson NJ, "Gasoline Alley" 227
Paul, Bob **172**
Pearson, Gil **41**, **46**, **48**, 49
Pennsboro WV 221

Penrose, Spencer 82
Permenter, George **100**
Perrung, Gil **301**
Perry, Len 220
Peterson, Jimmy **208**, **209**
Peterson, O.R. **233**
Peterson, Swan 288
Peterson, Tex **23**, **41**, **48**, 49
Peterson, Wild Pete **104**
Petillo, Kelly 105, 290, 291
Petticord, Jack **164**
Philadelphia PA, Fairmount Park, Belmont, Bygerry 215
Phillips, Jinx **115**
Phoenix AZ 88, 95
Picher OK, 116
Pickens, Bill 241
Piedmont Interstate Fairgrounds SC *see* Spartanburg SC
Pierson, Lindy **103**
Pigg, Troy **114**
Pikes Peak, CO 81, **82**, 170, 266
Pimlico Horse Track MD *see* Baltimore MD
Pingrey, W.H. 133
Pismo Beach CA 12, **22**, **23**
Pittsburgh PA, Brunots Island 215
Plankington SD 98
Plaucheville LA 243
Pleasanton CA **393**
Pompano FL 251
Portage La Prairie, Manitoba (Canada) 259
Portland OR 10
Portland OR, Base Line Speedway 11
Portland OR, Gresham Speedbowl 11, **36**
Portland OR, Portland Speedway 11, **300**, **302**
Portland OR, Rankin Track (Field) 16, **30**, **38**
Post Falls ID, Alan Track **77**
Powell, Al 253
Powell, Archie **135**
Powell, Leonard **180**
Powell OH **175**
Pratt, Brian 257
Prentiss, Fred **147**
Prescott AZ 89
Princess Anne VA *see* Norfolk VA
Pueblo CO 71
Pulver, Matt **94**

Quebec City, Quebec (Canada) 260
Quick, Sherman **22**
Quinn, Francis 266

Radbruch, Don **1**, **2**, 295, 296
Radbruch, Les 1
Raleigh NC 248
Ramascus, Rajah (Rajo Jack) 53
Ramono, E. Jean 266

Randall Park OH *see* Cleveland OH
Randolph, Dave 220
Rankin Track OR *see* Portland OR
Reading PA **155**, 215, **226**, 228, 234
Readville MA 192, **201**, **204**, **207**, **208**, **209**, 214
Real Road Racing 187
Records, Rex **225**, **238**
Redlands CA 14
Regina, Saskatchewan (Canada) 259, 267
Rehobeth Beach DE, Volunteer Speedway 221
Reid, Wallace **303**
Renner SD 98, **109**
Reno NV 68
Rhiley, King 81
Rhinebeck NY 192
Rice, Chuck **175**
Richmond VAw, Virginia State Fairgrounds 222
Richwine, Roy **237**
Rickenbacker, Eddie 44, 211
Rielly, Mike **52**
Riley, George 302
The Rim Riders *see* Hammond Speedway
Riverside Raceway CA 292
Roanoke Fairgrounds, VA 222
Roaring Roadsters 3
Roaring Roadsters #2 3
Roberts, Floyd, 7, **23**, 44, 45, **224**, 287
Robinson, Bob 249
Robson, George 63, **64**
Robson, Hal 63, **64**
Robson, Jimmy **64**
Roby IN, Roby Speedway 159, **161**, **162**, **163**
Rochester NY 192
Rockingham Motor Speedway *see* Salem NH
Rockingham Speedway *see* Salem NH
Rockville CT 193
Rocky Ford CO 71, 127
Rocky Mount NC 248
Rocky Mountain Midget Racing Association 131
Rogers, Billy **256**
Rogers, Hank **239**
Rogers, Louie **256**, **258**
Romeny WV 221
Rose, Bud (Harry Eisle) **46**, 63, **197**, 277
Rose, Mauri **169**, 187, **224**, **286**
Ross, Burt **208**
Ross, Jack 266
Roy, Gladys 288
Ruskin Track SD *see* Forestburg SD
Russo, Joe 105, **223**

318 Index

Rutherford, Slim 221
Rutland VT, Vermont State Fairgrounds 189

Saal, Tom 178
Sacramento CA, California State Fairgrounds 43
Sacramento CA, Hughes Stadium 7
Saint Cloud MN 98
St. Johns AZ 89
Saint Joseph MO 144
St. Louis MO, Maxwelliton Track 143
St. Paul MN 98, **106**, **108**
Salem IN 160
Salem NH, Rockingham Speedway, Rockingham Motor Speedway (Board Track) 189
Salem OR 11
Salina KS 113
Salinas CA 53
Salisbury MD 218
Sall, Bob **151**, **227**, **249**
Salt Lake City UT, Lagoon 68
Salt Lake City UT, Utah State Fairgrounds 68
San Antonio TX 92, 122
San Bernardino CA, Tri Cities Speedway **23**, **29**
San Diego CA, Neals Speedway **129**
San Diego CA, Neil's Sportsman Park 18
San Diego CA, Silvergate Speedway 18, **24**, **27**, **28**, **29**, **50**, **52**, **291**, **292**
San Francisco CA, Ingleside Track 11
San Francisco CA, 1915 Worlds Fair 12
San Francisco CA, San Francisco Motordrome 3
San Jose CA, San Jose Speedway 1, 3, **16**, **18**, **25**, **26**, **52**, **56**, **57**, **58**, **59**, **60**, **297**, **306**
San Luis Obispo CA 12, **13**, 14, **15**
Sands, Frank **100**
Sandusky OH 162
Santa Maria CA 12, 154
Sarles, Roscoe 159
Sarnia, Ontario (Canada) 259
Saulpaugh, Bryan 274, 275, 286
Saunders, Tex 48
Savannah GA 249, 250
Saylor, Everett **137**, **138**, **173**, **185**
Schindler, Bill **202**
Schlinder, Doris 203
Schneider, Lou **165**, **283**, **285**
Schock, Wally **42**
Schrader, Gus 25, 74, 75, 131, 132, 133, 139, **143**, **144**, 148, **149**, 182, 243, 292, 293
Schurch, Herman 223

Scollenberger, Dutch 229
Scottsdale AZ 89
Scovell, Bob **38**
Scovell, Vi 38
Seattle WA, Aurora Speedway (Speedbowl) 10, **35**, **39**, **66**
Seattle WA, Seattle Motor Speedway, Olympic View Speedway 10
Seattle WA, Seattle Municipal Stadium 10, **60**, 61
Secrets Magazine 3
Sedalia MO 143
Seim, Jimmy **269**
Seltzer, Robert **102**
Semans, Saskatchewan (Canada) 259
Sennett, Bud **48**
Senter Park NE *see* Franklin NE
Shafer, Red 71, 92
Shanoyian, Art 67
Sharon Speedway OH 162, **172**
Sharp, Jimmy 266
Shaw, Ben **243**
Shaw, Glen **303**
Shaw, Harold **197**
Shaw, Wilbur **163**, **166**, 274, 275, 285, 286, 290
Shearson, Bud 74
Sheepshead Bay NY, *see* Brooklyn NY
Sheffler, Bill 85
Sheldon CT 193
Sheldon CT, Huntington Speedway **198**
Shelley, Mr. **237**
Sheridan WY 68
Shickshinny PA 215
Shilling, Robert M. 55
Shreve, Don 122
Shreveport LA 242, **243**, 246, 247
Sidney MT 68
Silvergate Speedway CA *see* San Diego CA
Silverlake (Silver Lake) Speedway WA *see* Everett WA
Silvia, Bob 203, 213
Simmons, Ted **20**
Sioux City IA Interstate Fairgrounds 139, **141**
Sioux Falls SD, Sioux Empire Fairgrounds, Fred Buckmiller Race Track 98, **100**, **101**, **102**
Slattery, Jimmy **106**
Sloan, J. Alex 100, 139, 141, 163, 177, 178, 244, 245, 253, 254, 280, 288, 292, 296
Smith, Dudley 266
Smith, Jack **260**, **261**, 266
Smith, Jim 56, 57, **58**
Smithville MO 154
Snider, Dutch **60**
Snowberger, Russ 166, **237**, **238**
Snyder, Elvin 61
Snyder, Jimmy **150**

Soetaert, Bill 154
Somerset PA **219**
Sostillio, Joe **199**
Soulders, George 94, 95, 122
South Attleboro ME, Interstate Speedway Park **188**
South Bend IN 161, **176**
South Main TX *see* Houston TX
South Milwaukee Speedway *see* Milwaukee WI
South Gate CA, Southern Ascot Speedway 14, **61**, **62**, **63**, **86**, 392
Southwest Racing Association (SRA) 131
Sparks, Art **22**
Sparta Stadium IL *see* Chicago IL
Spartanburg SC, Spartanburg Fairgrounds, Piedmont Interstate Fairgrounds 249
Spaulding, Jack **264**
Speed Age 3, 253
Speed on Sand 253
Speedway Magazine **278**
Spence, Bill **21**, 138
Spencer WV 221
Spokane WA, Interstate Fair Grounds 9
Sprague, Clair 68
Springfield IL 141, 168, 202, 224
Springfield MO, Osark Empire Fair 144
Staneck, Eddie **201**
Stang, Herb **22**
Stapp, Babe **21**, 290
Staten Island NY, Bray Brook Oval 192
Staunton VA 222
Stein, Otis 229
Sterling IL **148**, **149**
Stevens, Jack **43**
Stevens, Myron **167**
Stewart, Art **218**
Stewart, George *see* Duray, Leon
Stone, Larry D. 81
Strong, Bill **31**, **33**
Stubblefield, Stubby **284**
Sturgis SD 82, 98
Suffolk VA 222
Sullivan, Larry 182
Sun Hawk, Chief **195**
Sun Prairie WI, Angell Park Speedway 139
Syracuse NY, New York State Fairgrounds 192, **200**, **204**

Tacoma WA 9
Talament, Sonny **162**
Tampa FL, Florida State Fairgrounds 251, **255**
Taylor, Jack 7, **23**, 267
Tegmeier, Fritz **169**
Tennessee State Fairgrounds *see* Nashville TN 241

Index

Termin, Joe **90**
Terre Haute IN, Black Demon Speedway **161**
Tetzlaff, Teddy **78**
Thistledowns OH *see* Cleveland OH
Thompson Speedway CT **194, 200, 225**
Tillamook OR **11**
Toft, Omar **10, 235**
Toledo OH, Fort Miami Speedway **152**
Topeka KS **113**
Toronto, Ontario (Canada), Canadian National Expo **259**
Trenton NJ, Inter-State Fairgrounds **215, 227**
Trepanier, Al **207**
Tri-Cities Speedway CA *see* San Bernardino CA
Triplett, Ernie **143, 145, 164, 287**
Troy Hills NJ **218, 220, 236, 237**
Tucson AZ **89**
Tulsa OK **115**
Tupelo MS, Mississippi-Alabama State Fairgrounds **243**
Turgeon, Henry **213**
Tuthill, Bill **253**

Ulesky, Johnny **237**
Union NJ **218, 227, 308**
Uniontown PA **235**
United States Auto Club (USAC) **6, 194**
Unser, Louie **170**
Urbana IL **141**
Utah State Fairgrounds *see* Salt Lake City UT

V.F.W. Speedway MI *see* Detroit MI

Vail, Ira **68, 156, 189, 211, 212**
Valasek, V. Ray **133, 138**
Valentine, Del **33**
Vancouver, British Columbia (Canada), Hastings Park **259, 266**
Vancouver WA **10, 11**
Vanderbilt Cup Races **221, 236**
Vanteight, Jerry **268**
Ventura CA **14**
Verbeck, Bob **76**
Vermont State Fairgrounds *see* Rutland VT
Vest, Chris **24**
Victoria, British Columbia (Canada), Colwood Park **260**
Victoria, British Columbia (Canada), Langford Speedway **52, 263, 264, 265, 266, 277, 268, 270, 272, 273**
Victoria, British Columbia (Canada), "On the Docks" **73, 267, 268, 269, 270, 271**

Virginia State Fairgrounds VI *see* Richmond VI
Voge, Don **102**
Volunteer Speedway DE *see* Rehobeth Beach DE
Vorbeck, Bob **121**

Waco TX **92, 246**
Wade, George **140**
Wade, George, Jr. **140**
Wagner, Eddie **107**
Wagner SD **98**
WaKeeney KS **113**
Walker, A.J. **288**
Walker, Bub **190**
Walker, Dorothy **288**
Walla Walla WA **10**
Wallace, Fred **13**
Wallard, Lee **182**
Walling, Claude **37**
Ward, Alan **277**
Warke, Buster **196**
Warner Park TN *see* Chattanooga TN **241**
Washington DC, Benning Speedway **218**
Washington, Oregon, Idaho Racing Association (WIORA) **86**
Washington PA, Arden Downs **220**
Waterloo IA **139**
Watertown NY **192**
Watson, Ed **122**
Watsonville CA **12, 295**
Wausau WI **139**
Way, J. Earl **234, 236**
Way, Jim **235**
Wearne, Frank **30, 44, 45, 65, 66**
Webb, Travis "Spider" **108, 174, 237**
Webster SD **100**
Weller, E.C. **133**
Wemester, Estan **161**
Wenneston, Esthan **141**
West, G.O. **113**
West, Harry **119**
West, Tex (Wetzler, Austin E) **90**
West, Tony **265**
West Sioux Falls SD **102, 106**
West Springfield MA, Eastern States Expo Speedway **193**
West Swansey NH, Hannahan Farm **189**
Western Racing Association (WRA) **56, 68**
Westside Track KS *see* Wichita KS
Weymouth MA **193, 199**
Wheeling Downs WV **221**
Where They Raced **187**
Whippet Special (Shaw) **163**
Whitehouse, Johnny **189**
Whitmer, Buck **151**
Wichita Falls TX **92**

Wichita KS, Westside Track, Meridian Speedway, Bo Sterns Track **113**
Wick, Lee **96, 97**
Wilburn, Jimmy (Jimmie) **30, 35, 131, 171, 243, 246, 261, 263, 265, 282**
Wilcox, H.C. **253**
Wilcox, Howdy **167**
Willets CA **12**
Williams Grove Speedway PA *see* Mechanicsburg PA
Williamson, Joe **34**
Williston ND **98**
Willkerson, Jimmy **65**
Willman, Tony **225**
The Willows, British Columbia (Canada) **260, 261, 262, 266**
Wilmington NC **248**
Wilson, Howard **153, 185**
Wilson, Ted **283**
Wilt, Dave **229, 230**
Winchester IN **159, 170, 171, 282**
Winchester VA **222**
Windsor CT **193**
Winfield, Ed **13, 17, 154**
Winfield KS **113**
Winn, Billy **105, 156, 168, 249, 285**
Winnipeg, Manitoba (Canada) **259**
Wisconsin Special **253, 254, 255**
Wohlfiel, Johnny **168, 186, 187**
Wonderlick, Eddie **58**
Wonderlick, Jerry **16, 80**
Wood, Bill **101**
Wood, Helen **102**
Wood, Jimmy **100, 101, 102, 106, 107, 137, 138**
Wood, Pearl **103**
Woodbridge NJ **218**
Woodbury, Cliff **146**
Woodford, Woody **32, 173**
Woods, Merritt "Pappy" **109**
Woonsocket Fairgrounds, RI **194**
Worcester MA **193**
Wright, Crocky **236, 237**
Wright, Johnny **266**

Yakima WA **10, 30, 31, 32, 33, 34, 36**
Yapp, Charlie **3**
Yates, Cecil **282**
Young, Leo **161**
Young, Paul **229, 230, 232, 233**
Youngish, Shorty **256**

Zarka, Gus **221**
Zimmer, Paul **185**
Zirtzman, L.M. **298**
Zohmer, Johnny (Border McKean) **229, 232**

www.ingramcontent.com/pod-product-compliance
Lightning Source LLC
Chambersburg PA
CBHW081538300426
44116CB00015B/2678